Macromedia Dreamweaver 8 How-Tos

100 Essential Techniques

David Karlins

Adobe Press

Macromedia Dreamweaver 8 How-Tos
100 Essential Techniques

This Adobe Press book is published by Peachpit

Peachpit
1249 Eighth Street
Berkeley, CA 94710
510/524-2178
800/283-9444
510/524-2221 (fax)

To report errors, please send a note to errata@peachpit.com
Peachpit is a division of Pearson Education

For the latest on Adobe Press books, go to www.adobepress.com
Copyright © 2007 by David Karlins

Editor: Becky Morgan
Production Editor: Jonathan Peck
Copyeditor: Joanne Gosnell
Technical Editor: Ann Navarro
Compositor: Danielle Foster
Indexer: Patti Schiendelman
Cover design: Maureen Forys
Interior design: Maureen Forys

ISBN 0-321-45072-8

9 8 7 6 5 4 3 2 1

Printed and bound in the United States of America

Dedication

Dedicated to my family, thanks for your support.

Acknowledgments

This book was made possible by valuable contributions from Becky Morgan, Jonathan Peck, and the entire editing, layout, and production team at Adobe Press and Peachpit. They created a challenging and supportive environment that produced a book I think readers will find readable, valuable, and fun. In writing this book, I drew—as always—on the insights, questions, discoveries, and complaints of my Dreamweaver students at San Francisco State University Multimedia Studies Program. That dynamic input allowed me to select 100 essential features of Dreamweaver, and explain how to use them in a way I am confident every reader will find clear and helpful. Most of all, I appreciate the support and contributions of my agent, Margot Maley Hutchison of the Waterside Agency, who gave birth to much more than this project.

Contents

CHAPTER ONE

Exploring the Dreamweaver Environment

Dreamweaver, with its multidimensional set of features for managing every aspect of Web and page design and management, has never been famous for an accessible environment. After five years of using and teaching Dreamweaver nearly every day, I continue to stumble on (or have students discover) time-saving techniques, hidden features, and better or more convenient ways to access frequently used techniques.

In this introductory chapter, I'll survey the key elements of the Dreamweaver interface and the best ways to access tools and features that you need to survive while you build a complex (or basic) Web site.

I won't waste our compact and precious space surveying features like Dreamweaver's Start Page. There's nothing wrong with the Start Page, but I'll assume that you're capable of clicking a link to a feature without my explaining that the link launches the feature. (Of course, I'll explain what these features *do* throughout the book.)

One of the joys of Dreamweaver 8 is that the unfortunate separation of the Mac and Windows versions that marred Dreamweaver MX 2004 has been rectified. While Dreamweaver 8 for OS X and Dreamweaver 8 for Windows each adopt the standards of the respective operating systems, they have the *same* features. The minor and understandable exception is the availability of a Homesite-type environment for Windows users, which I'll explain in #1, "Workspace Setup for Windows."

#1 Workspace Setup for Windows

Designing Pages in Code view or the Code Inspector

Dreamweaver 8's Document window provides three views: Code, Split, and Design. The Code and Split views are for developers who want to write their own markup code, rather than have Dreamweaver generate it. These views are covered in #2, "Exploring the Document Window."

Dreamweaver's Code Inspector window—available in both Windows and Mac versions—is accessed from the Window menu (Window > Code Inspector). The Code Inspector is a highly functional code-writing environment with a toolbar that provides prompts as you enter code, as well as prepackaged code snippets. The Code Inspector allows you to collapse or expand sections of coding, making it easier to focus on and edit sections of code.

Windows users launching Dreamweaver 8 for the first time will be prompted to choose between Designer and Coder workspaces. The Coder workspace is for page designers who want to write their own code—HTML (for page formatting) JavaScript (for animation and interactivity), CSS (for sitewide and page-specific formatting rules), and so on. Most people use Dreamweaver because they *don't want* to write their own code; they want to design page elements in a graphical environment and have *Dreamweaver* generate code for them. To take advantage of the code-generation capabilities of Dreamweaver, most users will want to choose the Designer workspace. And, of course, you can flip between views.

> **Tip**
> *The Coder workspace (not to be confused with Code view—which is available in both versions of Dreamweaver 8) is one of the few remaining differences between the Windows and Mac versions of Dreamweaver. Dreamweaver 8 for Windows and Dreamweaver 8 for Mac are essentially the same program. So why the Coder workspace for Windows? Just as humans have retained some anatomical attributes of our evolutionary ancestors, the two versions of Dreamweaver have minor differences due, in part, to the fact that Dreamweaver for Windows inherits a user base of designers who migrated to Dreamweaver through a Web design program called Homesite.*

Mainly to accommodate (former) Homesite designers, Dreamweaver for Windows provides the Coder workspace layout. When you launch Dreamweaver for Windows for the first time, the Workspace Setup dialog box prompts you to choose between the Designer and Coder layouts (**Figure 1a**).

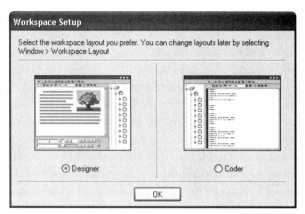

Figure 1a Choosing Designer view.

If, at any point, you want to switch to or from Code view in Dreamweaver 8 for Windows, choose Window > Workspace Layout > Designer to return to the normal Dreamweaver interface (**Figure 1b**).

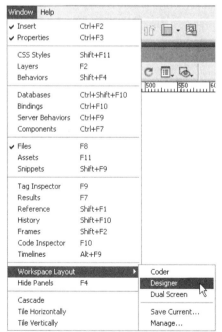

Figure 1b Choosing Designer mode.

2

Exploring the Document Window

Choosing a Document Type Definition (DTD)

Dreamweaver 8 uses XHTML 1.0 Transitional as the default document type for HTML Web pages. By generating XHTML-compatible coding for your Web page, you allow your Web page to integrate cutting-edge dynamic data content—content that is updated at a remote source and embedded (updated) in your Web page. Such dynamic data systems are issues that are decided at systemwide levels, not by a Web page designer. But again, by accepting Dreamweaver's default document type of XHTML 1.0 Transitional, you embed the ability to interact with and display dynamic data at any stage of system development.

The Document window is the basic workspace in Dreamweaver. The Document window is where you design Web pages; you can create or paste text, embed images, define links, or place and sometimes create page elements like style sheets (that control the look of a page), input forms, animation, and interactive objects (that react to actions by a visitor). In short, the Document window is where you will spend the bulk of your time in Dreamweaver. Even if you have some familiarity with creating pages in Dreamweaver, there are many features rooted within the various elements of the Document window, so it is worthwhile to explore them in some detail.

You'll see the Document window when you open an existing Web page or when you create a new one. Use the File menu to open an existing Web page (File > Open, or File > Open Recent to access a list of recently opened pages) or to create a new Web page (File > New).

When you choose File > New, the New Document dialog opens. Throughout this book we will explore some of the more useful Categories of new documents, but the first and main type of new document you'll create in the New Document dialog is a Basic page, and the basic and main type of Web page you'll create is an HTML page (**Figure 2a**).

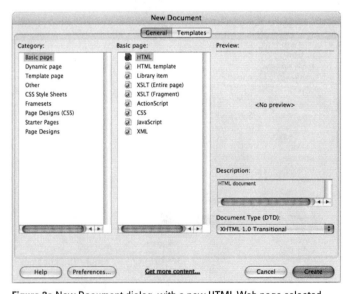

Figure 2a New Document dialog, with a new HTML Web page selected.

Clicking the Create button in the New Document dialog generates a new page, and opens that page in the Document window. As noted, the Document window is where you (and Dreamweaver) do the bulk of your work. As a result, the Document window is crammed with features. The objects floating around in the Document window are mainly panels, menus, and toolbars, which we'll explore in the following How-Tos in this chapter. But there are plenty of useful (and sometimes unintuitive) features in just the Document window that should be part of your design arsenal.

The Document window can display with three views: Code, Split, and Design. Code view displays *only* code, and is used by designers who wish to bypass Dreamweaver's ability to generate code. Design view hides most code, providing a graphical design interface. Split view displays code on the top of the Document window and a graphical design environment on the bottom (**Figure 2b**).

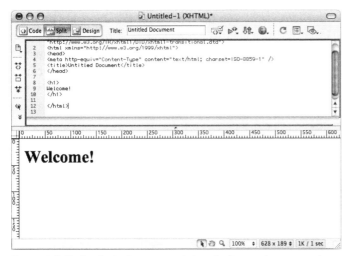

Figure 2b Split view in the Document window displays code on top and a graphical design interface on the bottom.

Create a Site Before Creating a Document

While you will spend the vast majority of your time with Dreamweaver in the Document window designing Web pages, the first step in creating a Web site is to define the *site*. Defining a local Web site ensures that, as you embed files in your Web pages, and as you define links between your Web pages, the connections between these linked files will be maintained.

Relying on Dreamweaver to manage links between your files becomes even more useful when you upload Web pages to an intranet or Internet site.

If you are stepping into a Web design project in which the local Dreamweaver site has already been defined, you can create additional pages within that site without worrying about the site definition. If you are starting a new Web site from scratch, you should define your site before saving Web pages. See Chapter 3, "Defining a Web Site," for details on how to define a local Web site. See Chapter 4, "Connecting to a Remote Server," for information on how to connect that local site to a remote site.

There are a number of advantages to working in Split view, especially for designers who are not comfortable or proficient in writing their own code. Split view is a way to familiarize yourself with coding, since generated code appears as you create elements in the graphical design window. And, even though Dreamweaver is the best existing program for generating HTML and other page layout code, there are times when the only way to troubleshoot a design problem is to edit the code directly. If you edit code in Split view, you can see the effect by clicking in the lower (graphical) window.

Stripped of menus and panels, the main features available in the Document window are rulers, the tag selector, and the status bar. Horizontal and vertical rulers provide a quick way to judge the size of your page and objects on it. Hide or change ruler attributes by choosing View > Rulers from the menu. The View > Rulers submenu lets you show or hide rulers and change the unit of measurement from the default pixels to centimeters or inches.

The tag selector, on the left side of the status bar on the bottom of the Document window, allows you to select specific tags for editing in the Property Inspector (the Property Inspector is examined in #3, "Viewing Panels and the Property Inspector"). It is especially handy when you're working with objects like tables or embedded CSS (page design objects), and simply clicking an object in the Document window itself can be difficult.

The right side of the status bar has some handy and exciting tools that are new to Dreamweaver 8.

- The Select and Hand tools provide two ways to navigate around your document—with the Hand tool working like similar tools in Photoshop or Illustrator—allowing you to grab a section of the page and drag it in or out of view.

- The Zoom tool is a long-demanded way to draw a marquee and enlarge a section of a page.

- The Set Magnification drop-down menu is another way to define magnification.

- The Window size display tells you the size of your design window—normally in pixels.

- The File Size/Download Time display estimates download time for the page parameters (**Figure 2c**).

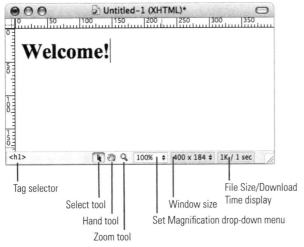

Tag selector

Select tool

Hand tool

Zoom tool

File Size/Download Time display

Window size

Set Magnification drop-down menu

Figure 2c The tag selector and status bar.

Setting Connection Speed

When you define download speed in the Status Bar category of the Preferences dialog, you can choose from presets in the drop-down menu. Oddly enough, these presets don't include many typical download speed options, like 256 kilobits per second, which is the current standard for DSL or cable Internet connections. To define a custom download speed, simply type a value into the Connection speed box.

You can adjust the units displayed for window size, or the connection speed used to estimate download time in the Status Bar category of the Preferences dialog. On the Mac, choose Dreamweaver > Preferences, and in Windows choose Edit > Preferences, and then select the Status Bar category to edit these parameters (**Figure 2d**).

Figure 2d Editing status bar parameters.

#3 Viewing Panels and the Property Inspector

Many of the features explored in other chapters and How-Tos in this book are available in *panels*—rectangular boxes that are normally aligned to the right of the Document window. While each panel obviously controls different features of your Web site or Web pages, panels have some features in common.

Dreamweaver panels all provide access to very different features. But there are display elements common to all panels (**Figure 3a**).

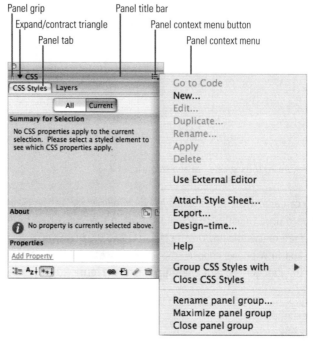

Figure 3a Elements of Dreamweaver panels.

You can drag panels from their default position on the right side of the Document window by dragging on the Panel grip.

You can separate tabbed panels by choosing Group Assets with from the Panel context menu, and then choosing New panel group (**Figure 3b**).

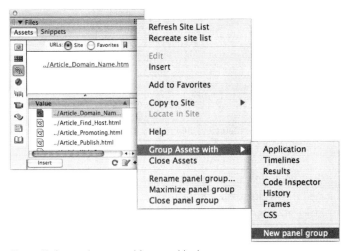

Figure 3b Separating a panel from a tabbed group.

Similarly, group panels with other panels as tabbed groups by choosing Group Assets with from the Panel context menu and selecting another panel to which the selected panel will be grouped.

You can expand or contract panels using the Expand/contract triangle. To hide (or unhide) all open panels, press the F4 function key.

Display panels by selecting them from the Window menu. Active panels display with check marks next to them in the Window menu.

The Properties panel—usually called the Property inspector—is a unique and special type of panel. It is adaptive in that it allows you to edit properties of a selected object, somewhat similar to the Object bar in many Adobe applications. For example, if you select text, the Property Inspector makes available options for formatting type, including type size, type font, type style, and link attributes (**Figure 3c**).

Other Uses of the Property Inspector

You will likely use the Property Inspector mainly to apply attributes to text and images. But the Property Inspector also adapts to and provides formatting options for other selected page elements.

If you select a table, you can define table size, number of columns, number of rows, cell padding (space between cell content and the edge of a cell), cell spacing (space between cells), table background color, and other attributes. If you select a table *cell*, you can define horizontal and vertical alignment, cell width and height, cell background color, and other alignment and color attributes.

Input forms and their embedded form fields have attributes that can be edited in the Property Inspector as well.

More complex page design elements like Div tags and Layers also have definable attributes that can be edited in the Property Inspector.

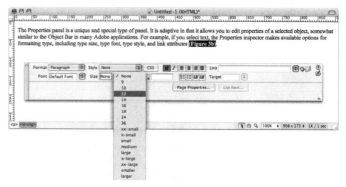

Figure 3c With text selected, the Property inspector allows you to define type attributes.

Or, if you select an image, the Property inspector makes available image formatting attributes, like image size, ALT text (alternate text to make your image accessible to visitors or browsers who cannot view images), or hotspots (clickable linked areas within an image).

#4 Examining the Standard and Document Toolbars

Many of Dreamweaver's page design tools are most easily accessed through toolbars. The Standard toolbar has some basic tools that are common to almost any application. The Document toolbar, on the other hand, provides access to an underappreciated set of rather powerful page design and management tools. The toolbars reside at the top of the Document window, and are displayed (if they are hidden) by choosing them from the View > Toolbars menu.

The tools in the Standard toolbar allow you to create new files, open existing files, print code, copy, cut, paste, and undo or redo an action. All these features are accessible from either the File or Edit menus (**Figure 4a**).

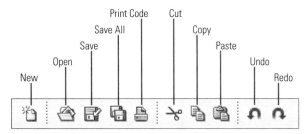

Figure 4a The Standard toolbar.

The Document toolbar collects some of the most frequently used tools used for page design and management. The three buttons on the left allow you to toggle between Code, Split, and Design view (these views are discussed for both Mac and Windows users in #1, "Workspace Setup for Windows."

The Document toolbar also provides a convenient way to define a page *title*—the page "name" that displays in the title bar of a visitor's browser. You define a page title by typing the text to be displayed as a title in the Title box in the Document toolbar.

Page Title and Page File Name

Every Web page has both a filename and a page title. The filename is the "internal" name—the way the file is identified and located within a Web site, and the way browsers find the file. Filenames must be supported by Web servers, and therefore developers often avoid special characters and stick to alphanumeric characters and lowercase in defining page filenames. While filenames are not the main or most obvious way visitors will identify a page, they're not hidden or secret, which should be kept in mind when assigning filenames.

Page *titles* are not part of the process of identifying or linking a file; they are an attribute of the page that describes or summarizes the page content for visitors. They *can* contain special characters, including punctuation and spaces.

As noted, *every* page has a page title, but unless you assign a page title, the default "Untitled Page" page title appears in browser title bars.

The rest of the Document toolbar tools are used for managing documents, document display, and file management (**Figure 4b**).

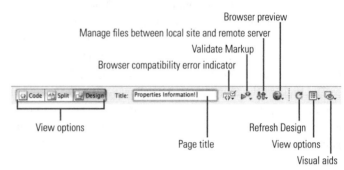

Figure 4b Entering a page title in the Document window.

The browser compatibility error indicator display is based on options you choose in the Validate Markup tool menu. You can choose from a variety of Web standards in the Settings menu available from this tool, and then choose actions (validating the open document, selected files, or all of the files in your site).

The File Management tool is a shortcut for managing files between your local computer and a remote server. Site management is explored in detail in Chapter 4, "Connecting to a Remote Server."

The Preview in Browser tool allows you to see how your page will look in a browser window. View options include displaying (or hiding) rulers, guides, and grids. Visual Aids include displaying borders of tables, frames, and CSS objects—borders that are not displayed in browsers, but are handy for design purposes.

#5 Viewing Style Rendering Tools

The Style Rendering toolbar is another exciting, CSS designer-friendly innovation in Dreamweaver 8. With the advent of Dreamweaver MX 2004, Dreamweaver made Cascading Style Sheets (CSS) the default method for applying formatting to type. When you choose type attributes in the Property Inspector, Dreamweaver generates CSS code instead of older, less-flexible HTML formatting attributes.

The Style Rendering toolbar (**Figure 5**) facilitates quick toggling between "bare" type (and other elements) and viewing the page with CSS formatting applied. Bare type is type stripped of all formatting (colors, fonts, adjusted font sizes, line spacing, etc.). This allows you to easily isolate and work on page content and see page content as it will display in browsing environments that do not support CSS formatting.

Note

Browsing environments that don't support CSS formatting (or that apply different CSS formatting than that defined by the Web designer) include browsers configured for handicapped viewers (including people with various vision disabilities), devices like cell phones or PDAs that do not support a full set of CSS formatting options, or devices where the user has elected to enforce their own style choices for personal reasons.

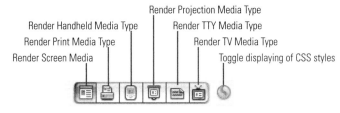

Render Projection Media Type
Render Handheld Media Type — Render TTY Media Type
Render Print Media Type — Render TV Media Type
Render Screen Media — Toggle displaying of CSS styles

Figure 5 The Style Rendering toolbar.

The Style Rendering toolbar also allows you to toggle between viewing digital and print formatting.

Printable CSS

By providing an alternate page (or site) style sheet for *printing*, you can allow visitors to generate a printer-friendly version of your page that displays differently than the Web version of the page.

Tip
Dreamweaver allows you to generate separate sets of styles (CSS) for digitally displayed content (viewed on a monitor) and print output. Generating CSS files for onscreen and print display are discussed in #56, " Creating and Updating an External Style Sheet File"

You can define additional CSS files for use with handheld media, projection media (Web pages projected in full-screen slide-show format), TTY format (media output that requires font defined in points, not pixels), or TV media type.

#6 Using the Insert Toolbars

The Insert toolbars are the ubiquitous blue-collar power tools of Dreamweaver. As these toolbars provide access to the bulk of Dreamweaver's features, many developers keep them displayed at all times for quick access to features that can also be found, less conveniently, in Menu options or panels. Since a large percentage of Dreamweaver features, ranging from everyday (inserting images) to esoteric (detailed database management) are accessible from the nine basic tabs in the Insert toolbars, they will be invoked throughout this book. Here, the point is to get comfortable with how the Insert toolbar works.

The Insert toolbars are a *set* of toolbars. You get the whole package: Common, Layout, Forms, Text, HTML, Application, Flash elements, and Favorites.

To display the Insert toolbars, choose View > Toolbars > Insert. By default, the Insert toolbars display in Menu form—you use a drop-down menu to switch between the eight different iterations of the toolbar (**Figure 6a**).

Figure 6a Choosing from the set of Insert toolbars.

To view all Insert toolbars at once, as a tabbed version of the toolbar, choose Show as Tabs from the toolbar menu. In tab view, you can easily switch between the eight different toolbars by clicking a tab (**Figure 6b**).

Figure 6b The Insert toolbars, displayed as tabs.

To get back to untabbed menu view, choose Show as Menu from the Insert toolbar context menu (**Figure 6c**).

Figure 6c Toggling from tab view to menu view.

While a full survey of the options in the Insert toolbars would amount to a documentation of most of the features available in Dreamweaver, I'll point you to some of the easy-to-access features in each Insert toolbar:

- Common: Define links, e-mail links, page links (anchors), tables, and media.

- Layout: Create the three main modes for page design in Dreamweaver—tables, Div tags, and Layers.

- Forms: Define input forms, form fields, and form-handling buttons.

- Text: Apply HTML styles to text and insert special characters.

- HTML: Define useful metatags like keywords and descriptions for search engines.

- Application: Manage dynamic data from a linked data source.

- Flash elements: Insert Flash objects.

- Favorites: A customizable bar; Ctrl + Click to add features.

CHAPTER TWO

Controlling the Dreamweaver Document Window

You will spend most of your time in Dreamweaver working in the Document window. The Document window is where you enter (or paste copied) text, embed images, design your page, apply formatting, and even add animation, video, interactive elements, and forms. In short, most of the features covered in the rest of this book are available through the Document window. The techniques in this chapter will explain in more detail how to navigate in and take advantage of the different editing and viewing options in the Document window.

You can work on and edit pages in three modes in the Document window. Code view is for writing HTML, JavaScript, and Cascading Style Sheets (CSS) by hand. Design view is for creating and formatting page elements and having Dreamweaver translate those elements into code. Split view splits the Document window between Code and Design views. You can *roughly* simulate how a page will look in a viewing environment by choosing a Media type (such as print, computer monitor, or handheld device) from the Style Rendering toolbar. For the most precise preview, use the Preview in browser icon/menu in the Document toolbar. In this chapter, you'll learn to take advantage of all these viewing options.

#7 Three Ways to Edit Page Content

There are three ways to *edit* the content of a Web page in Dreamweaver's Document window: Code view, Split view, or Design view. Even if you never plan to enter a line of code, it is helpful to understand how these three views work and how to take advantage of them.

Most page designers do most of their work in Design view. Design view allows you to apply page design formatting and add content to your page in an environment that looks like a word processor. As you enter text, embed images, or apply formatting—using graphical design tools—Dreamweaver generates the necessary code. The easiest way to see how this works is in Split view. In Split view, the top of the screen displays generated code, and the bottom of the screen displays the graphical design interface (**Figure 7**).

At the bottom of the screen in Split view (or on the entire screen in Design view), Dreamweaver displays a representation of how that code will be interpreted in a browser. This can only be an approximation, as different browsers and different versions of browsers display code differently. Dreamweaver 8 provides two approaches to seeing more accurate previews of your page in different browsing environments; you can use the tools in the Style Rendering toolbar, or click the Preview/Debug in Browser button in the Document toolbar.

When you define page elements in Design view, your work is translated into code that is interpreted by browsers. When you enter code into Code view, that code is translated into a graphical display in Design view. If you enter code into the Code view of the

Document window, the Design view updates when you switch to Design view. Or, if you are in Split view, changes to code update in the Design window when you click in the window.

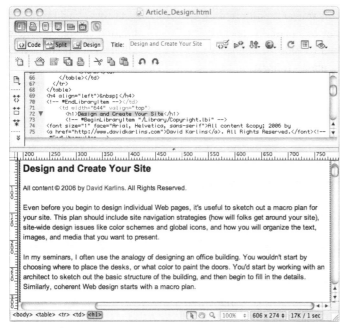

Figure 7 In Split view, the top of the screen displays code and the bottom of the screen displays a graphic simulation of how that code will display in a browser.

Examining Page Designs

By examining other sites' page code, you can explore techniques used by other designers. You can do this by copying the source code for the page into Dreamweaver. This works whether or not you know what the source code means. To copy source code from a Web page, choose View > Source in your browser. (The command might differ slightly depending on your browser.)

After you open the page's source code in a browser window, press Command + A (Mac)/Ctrl + A (Windows) to select all the code, and then press Command/Ctrl + C to copy it to the clipboard.

Back in Dreamweaver, choose File > New to open the New Document dialog. Choose Basic Page in the Category list, then choose HTML as the Basic Page type, and click Create.

With your new blank page open, click the Code View tab in the Document toolbar. Select the existing code, and press Command/Ctrl + V to paste the code you copied from another page into Dreamweaver. You will paste over the original code.

Finally, you can see the underlying page structure of the page you copied by clicking the Design tab in the Document toolbar.

#8 Managing the Design Window

The Style Rendering toolbar at the top of the Document window can be displayed (or hidden) by choosing View > Toolbars, and then selecting (or deselecting) the Style Rendering toolbar (**Figure 8a**). The Style Rendering toolbar allows you to preview how your page will appear on different kinds of viewing devices, from printed output to handheld devices. The Style Rendering toolbar also allows you to hide all applied CSS styles. CSS styles are the main way of applying formatting to Web pages.

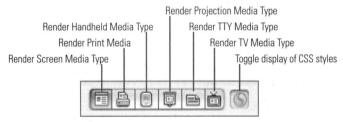

Render Projection Media Type
Render Handheld Media Type   Render TTY Media Type
Render Print Media   Render TV Media Type
Render Screen Media Type   Toggle display of CSS styles

Figure 8a The Style Rendering toolbar allows you to preview page display in a variety of output options ranging from print to handheld devices.

The options you choose from the Style Rendering toolbar *approximate* how a page will look in a browser. Some formatting features do not display in any version of Design view. For example, defined links change their display (usually change color) depending on whether or not they have been visited. By default, visited links are purple, and unvisited links are blue. However, the visited link state does not appear in the Design window.

For the most exact preview of how a page will look in a browser, use Dreamweaver's Preview in Browser tool, which is found in the Document toolbar (**Figure 8b**).

Figure 8b Choosing a browser from the Preview in Browser tool in the Document toolbar.

You can add browsers to the set that appears in the Preview in Browser list. The browsers you add must already be installed on your computer. To add a browser to the list, choose Edit Browser List from the Preview in Browser drop-down menu. This opens the Preview in Browser category in the Preferences dialog. Click the plus symbol (+) to open the Add Browser dialog. Click the Browse button in the dialog, and navigate to the application file for the browser program you wish to add. You can select a check box in the Preferences dialog to define a browser as Primary or Secondary. However, such definitions are not too important because you can select any available browser from the Preview in Browser tool.

Tip

Professional Web designers install the widest possible selection of browsers and preview Web pages on every available browser.

One important option in the Preview in Browser panel in the Preferences dialog (**Figure 8c**) is the Preview Using Temporary File check box. Selecting this option allows you to preview files in a browser window before or without transferring the page to a Web server. This is a helpful option.

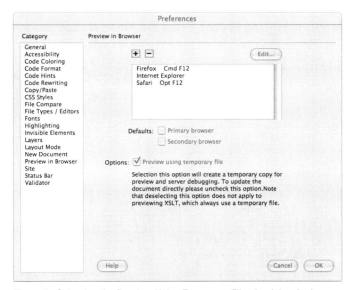

Figure 8c Selecting the Preview Using Temporary File check box in the Preview in Browser panel in the Preferences dialog.

#8: Managing the Design Window

#9 Arranging Windows

Both the Mac and Windows versions of Dreamweaver 8 support displaying multiple open pages as tabs. Jumping between open pages by clicking tabs is much easier than using the Window menu to navigate between open pages as you edit (**Figure 9a**).

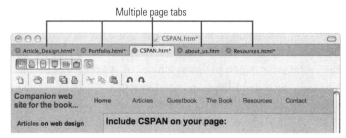

Figure 9a Several open pages displayed as tabs.

Tabbed pages that have not been saved display with an asterisk (*). You can close a page by clicking the small circle on the page tab.

If you prefer to view pages in their own windows, choose Window > Cascade to break pages into movable windows. To tile pages, choose Window > Tile (**Figure 9b**). To return to tabbed pages, choose Window > Combine as Tabs.

Figure 9b You can move cascaded pages separately.

#10 Controlling Display from the Status Bar

A new and substantially underrated feature of Dreamweaver 8 is the customizable, helpful display of information in the Document window Status Bar. You'll find the Status Bar at the bottom of the window (**Figure 10a**). This helpful feature often provides the best way to select an element of a page to edit in Design view. The Select tool and Hand tool provide navigation and selection control, which was not available in previous versions of Dreamweaver. Magnification is a truly radical innovation in page design technique. Also, the window size and download time indicators provide quick access to projecting how your page will look and how long it will take to appear in different browsing environments.

Using Zoom to Preview Projection

While most browsing environments do not support zooming, zooming has an important use in previewing Web pages that will be projected. With the proliferation of reasonably priced, widely available digital projectors, many Web pages end up projected on a screen. Zooming in on images is a way to preview how such graphics will look when projected on a large screen.

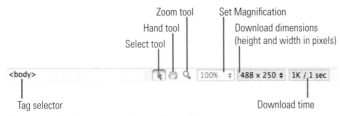

Figure 10a The Document window Status Bar.

As you create complex elements on your page, the tag selector becomes indispensable in selecting those elements. For example, if you just click in the Document window and use a table as a page layout tool, it's often difficult to distinguish between selecting a table cell embedded in a table and selecting the table itself. Even if you're unfamiliar with code or HTML, you can often identify a tag like "table" with an element on the page (a table) and select that object in the tag selector section of the Status Bar window (**Figure 10b**).

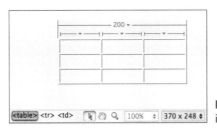

Figure 10b Selecting a table in the tag selector.

Note

Formatting with tables is covered in Chapter 6, "Page Layout with Tables."

The Hand, Select, and Zoom tools work like their cousins in programs like Photoshop and Illustrator. Use the Hand tool to drag the page around in the Document window. Use the Select tool (which is the default mode) to select objects on the page.

Until Dreamweaver 8, zooming and magnification were not options for Web page designers. While most browsers do not support zooming or magnification, these tools are helpful when you are aligning objects or inspecting images.

One of the ongoing challenges for Web page designers is anticipating how a Web page will look in various-sized browser windows. The Window size pop-up menu has several common browser-window-dimension presets, and you can click the Edit Sizes menu choice to open the Status Bar panel in the Preferences dialog and define additional presets.

Similarly, Web designers need to be aware of page file size and download time (**Figure 10c**). Large file sizes, of course, take longer to download. It's easy to add large image or media files without anticipating how it can strain a visitor's patience as he or she waits for the page content to download. An occasional glance at the Status Bar will reconnect you with reality and help you keep file size reasonable. You can define a connection speed on which download time is based by choosing Edit Sizes from the Download Dimensions/Download Time drop-down menu.

Setting Connection Speeds

Oddly, the default connection speed options in the Status Bar panel of the Preferences dialog do not include many typical download speeds for residential cable or DSL connections (like 256 or 384 kbs). However, you can simply enter a value in the Connection speed box.

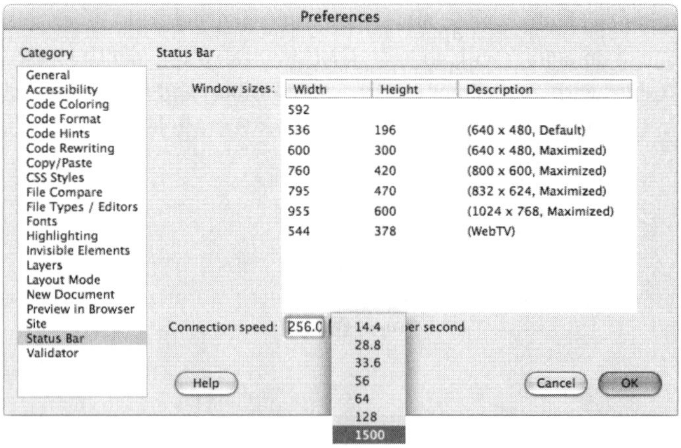

Figure 10c You can edit the connection speed in the Status Bar category of Preferences.

Controlling the Dreamweaver Document Window

CHAPTER THREE

Defining a Web Site

Many people think of Web design in terms simply of creating a Web *page*. However, a Web *site* is a fundamental part of a Web page. A Web site allows pages to connect to each other with links. It makes it possible to embed images or other nontext content in pages. Your Web site can include (usually one, but sometimes more) style sheet files that control the formatting of multiple pages across a site.

Dreamweaver has essentially two work environments—the Design window and the Files window. The Files window provides tools to control your Web site.

Defining a Dreamweaver Web site is necessary to manage your files and make them all work together. It is also necessary when you get ready to transfer your site content from your local computer to a remote server—where others can access your content.

Note

Defining a remote server connection and transferring files to and from a remote server is covered in Chapter 4, "Connecting to a Remote Server."

Dreamweaver 8 also has tools that allow you to manage your files once you define your site. When you move or rename a Web page (or any file in your site) Dreamweaver updates any links that are affected by that change.

Finally, in this chapter, you'll explore the somewhat underrated tools in Dreamweaver 8 for generating and saving graphical site maps that display pages and links. These site maps are a valuable way to manage site links or share an overview of a Web site.

#11 Collecting Site Content

The most basic elements of Web site content are text and images. But the Web is rapidly becoming more accessible and friendly to other types of content—media files, Adobe PDF files, FlashPaper files, and other types of content are increasingly moving to the "accessible" list. Content beyond text and images, however, requires plug-in software—programs like Flash Player, QuickTime player, Windows Media Player, Adobe Reader, and other programs that *add* capacity to browsers.

Web browsers can interpret and display text and images without plug-ins. For this reason, and because a large percentage of Web site content remains text and images, this How-To will focus on preparing text and images for your site.

The *most accessible* Web content is HTML text. HTML stands for HyperText Markup Language—the "hyper" referring not to drinking too many caffeinated beverages, but to the fact that Web text includes *links*—clickable text (or images).

Not all formatting features work the same way on a Web page as they do on a printed page. This poses a challenge when you copy or import text into Dreamweaver.

> **Note**
>
> *Technically speaking, bringing text intended for a printed page into a Web page involves translating the formatting from PostScript (the coding language used for most printing) into HTML (the markup language used for formatting Web text).*

Preparing text for Web pages requires bridging the gap between formatting markup language that translates into print formatting (usually PostScript), and formatting markup language that is supported by Web pages. There are several ways to move text to a Web page, but none of them are completely satisfactory. This is because type formatting in a word processor, like Microsoft Word, has features that are not available in Web formatting, and vice versa.

There are three basic options for bringing type to a Web page:

- Copying relatively unformatted text into Dreamweaver, and formatting it in Dreamweaver.

- Using export tools in your word processor, and import tools in Dreamweaver to translate the markup language from PostScript to HTML.

- Saving the text file as an Adobe PDF or FlashPaper file, opening the file in a browser using plug-in software, and defining links to the file in a Dreamweaver Web page.

Note

The third option, saving text files as FlashPaper or PDF files, is explored in detail in Chapter 13, #72, "Including FlashPaper Objects and PDF Files in Your Site."

There are important advantages to using the first two options listed above. If you copy and paste text from your word processor into Dreamweaver, you can avail yourself of all the formatting tools provided by Dreamweaver. These tools are designed to apply formatting that can be interpreted well and consistently by browsers. The downside of this method is that you'll need to reapply formatting in Dreamweaver.

On the other hand, saving your word processing file as an HTML file (some word processors have a Save As Web Page option) allows you to bring as much formatting as possible with the text as you move it into Dreamweaver. The downside of this method is that the formatting generated by your word processor is unlikely to hold up as consistently in browsers as text formatted in Dreamweaver.

Tip

If you're not using Word, other word processors like TextEdit, WordPerfect, and OpenOffice all save to Word format.

The Windows version of Dreamweaver allows you to import Word (and Excel) files directly to Web pages. This saves the step of opening the file in a word processor and saving it as an HTML file. To import a Word or Excel file, open the Web page to which you are importing the file, and choose File > Import > Word Document (or Excel Document). The Import Document dialog opens, and you can choose a few options for importing, ranging from Text Only (no formatting) to Text with Structure Plus Full Formatting (which retains the most formatting) (**Figure 11a**).

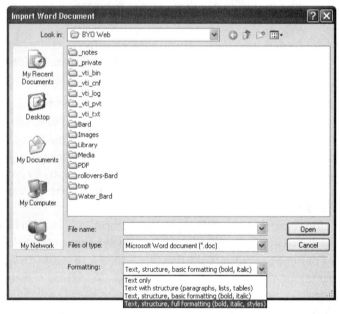

Figure 11a Importing a Word file in the Windows version of Dreamweaver.

There is a technique for moving text into Web pages that allows you to maintain basic formatting markup without forcing formatting into HTML from PostScript that really doesn't work well on Web pages. This technique is to rely on *styles* applied to type, not set formatting. For instance, in Word, you would use Heading 1, Heading 2, and so on, to define different styles of type. These word processing *styles* will come into Dreamweaver as HTML tags when you save your document as a Web page. Then the type will adopt the formatting attributes applied to your Web site style—attributes that work well in browsers.

Note
For a full exploration of creating, applying, and editing CSS styles, see Chapter 11, "Formatting Page Elements with CSS."

If you save a Word file as an HTML page, or if you use the Windows-only option for importing a Word file into a Dreamweaver Web page, you can clean up the HTML that results by choosing Commands > Clean Up Word HTML. From the Clean up HTML from popup menu, choose a version of Word and accept the default check box settings to strip coding from the generated HTML that will confuse browsers (**Figure 11b**).

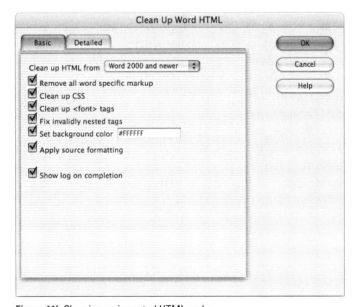

Figure 11b Cleaning up imported HTML code.

Differences Between Print and Web Images

Preparing images for the Web presents a separate set of challenges. There are several major differences between images and on the Web and images prepared for print documents. These differences include:

- Web images are usually saved at 72 dpi (dots per inch), while print images are routinely saved at 300 dpi and higher resolution.

- Web images are saved using the RGB (Red, Green, Blue) color system, while print images usually use CMYK (Cyan, Magenta, Yellow, Black) color mode.

- Web images are saved to JPEG, GIF, or PNG format, while print images are often saved in the TIFF format.

Programs like Adobe Illustrator, Adobe Photoshop, and Photoshop Elements have Save for Web features that can assist you in preparing images for the Web.

Many programs, (Adobe Photoshop and Photoshop Elements being the most prominent) allow you to export image files to JPEG, GIF, or PNG format. These programs provide you with advice on when to use which format. Here, I'll list a few basic attributes of the various formats:

JPEG images support millions of colors and are best for photographs. *Progressive* JPEG files "fade in" as they download, rather than appearing line by line.

GIF images support far fewer colors than the JPEG format, and are not usually used for photos. But GIF images support *transparency,* which allows the background of a Web page to show through empty spots in the image. GIF images can be defined as *interlaced.* Interlacing, like the progressive attribute in JPEG images, allows the image to fade in as it downloads.

PNG images support more colors, like JPEG, and allow you to define a transparent color, like GIF files. However, PNG format is generally not acceptable for photos because it lacks the JPEG format's capacity to manage colors and photo detail.

Programs like Photoshop allow you to preview how images will look in all three formats, with different settings for quality. Higher quality preserves color and image quality. But higher-quality images (and larger ones) take longer to download than small or lower-quality images.

Lower-quality images are generated using *compression.* Compression "looks for" pixels in an image that do not need to be saved as part of the file information, and it reduces file size by saving less of the image definition.

#12 Defining a Local Site

"I'm a designer, not a file manager!" I hear this protest each time I teach Dreamweaver, and I sympathize. But you need a *basic* understanding of how Web sites manage and organize files, or your site will fall apart. Links won't work, embedded images won't appear in pages, media files won't open, and style sheets, which control page format, won't attach.

The good news is that Dreamweaver will manage all your file connection issues, as long as you play by a few simple rules. The first of these rules is: *always start by defining a Dreamweaver Web site.* This Web site will manage your files for you. If you change a filename, Dreamweaver will update links throughout your site. If you go on an organizing binge and decide to move all your images into appropriate file folders, Dreamweaver will update links throughout your Web site. Again, to emphasize: This works as long as you 1) set up a Dreamweaver Web site, and 2) do *all* your file management (renaming or moving files) in the Dreamweaver Site panel.

Now that I've emphasized the importance of creating a local site, here's how you do it:

1. Start by collecting all your site content in a single folder. You can create subfolders (subdirectories) for images, media, Web pages, and so on. But all these folders must be within the folder that will serve as your local site folder.

2. From the Document window menu, choose Site > New Site. The Site Definition dialog opens.

continued on next page

3. At the top of the dialog, click the Advanced tab to see all options at once, instead of a wizard that reveals only one element of the site at a time. In the Category list, choose Local Info (**Figure 12**).

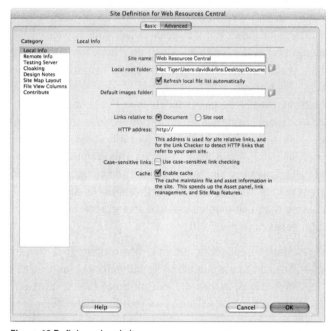

Figure 12 Defining a local site.

4. In the Site name box, enter any text you wish. Nobody will see this but you and other developers; it is simply descriptive information to help you remember which Web site this is.

5. In the Local root folder area, click the folder at the right and navigate to the folder in which you saved all your files.

6. If you want Dreamweaver to automatically save images to one folder on your local storage system (usually a hard drive), you can navigate to a folder using the folder icon next to the Default images folder field. This is not a particularly essential option, and it can get in your way if you want to make conscious decisions on where files are stored.

7. Choose the Links relative to Document radio button; this is the most efficient and reliable way to generate and update links between files, and to define links for embedded images.

8. The only other important option is the Enable cache check box. This activates the Asset panel that displays all site content.

9. With your local site defined, click OK. Dreamweaver is now ready to organize your files for you.

Transferring Files to a Remote Server Requires a Defined Local Site

In the techniques in Chapter 4, you'll learn how to connect to, and transfer files to and from a remote site. That site—either a Web server or a local intranet server—will make your site content available to the world (or, in the case of an intranet server, to a select group of users).

When you define your remote site, you can add a URL for the site to the local site panel in the HTTP Address field of the Site Definition dialog. But this information is not necessary to begin designing your Web site.

#13 Organizing Site Files and Folders

When it's time for housekeeping and moving files from one folder to another, you can also rely on the Dreamweaver Files panel. You can display the Files panel by choosing Window > File, or pressing the F8 function key (to toggle between displaying and hiding the Files panel).

The Files panel menu has options for typical file management actions, like creating new files or folders, renaming files, copying or pasting files, deleting files, and so on (**Figure 13a**).

Figure 13a Using the Files panel menu to create a subfolder in a selected folder.

The theme of this technique is as essential as it is simple: *Never* change filenames or move files between folders using your operating system's file management tools. Instead, *always* rely on Dreamweaver's Files panel to manage filenames and to move files between folders. The Site folder looks and works like the Finder (for Mac) or Explorer (for Windows) utilities. It allows you to drag files between folders, copy and paste files, rename files, and delete files, just as you would do in Finder or Explorer.

Why should you use Dreamweaver's Files panel? Because in a Web site, files are almost always connected to other files. You might have an image embedded in a page. If you change the name of that image file or move it to another folder, the link between that image and the page in which it is embedded becomes corrupted.

However, if you do all your file management in Dreamweaver, Dreamweaver will *fix* the problems caused by moving or renaming a file by redefining links that involve that file. For instance, if files in your Web site contain links to a file and that filename is changed,

Dreamweaver will prompt you to change those links in an Update Files dialog (**Figure 13b**).

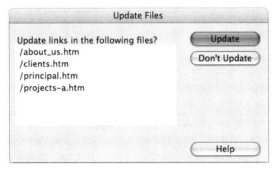

Figure 13b Dreamweaver redefining links to match a changed filename.

When you define your local Web site in Dreamweaver (see #12, "Defining a Local Site"), you define a local site folder. Dreamweaver knows that this folder is where all your site files *should be* kept. If you open a file from another folder or embed a file from another folder, Dreamweaver will prompt you to save a copy of that file in your Web folder. For example, if you embed an image in a Web page, Dreamweaver will prompt you to save that image to your site file when you place it on the page (**Figure 13c**).

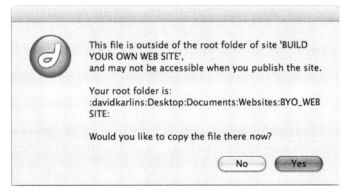

Figure 13c Dreamweaver prompts you to save a file of embedded images in the Web site folder.

#13: Organizing Site Files and Folders

#14 Prototyping Site Navigation

Skilled Web designers create Web pages with a clear plan for how those pages will be accessed. From what page will they be linked? To what pages will they link? The system of links between pages defines a site navigation structure. Such a structure is like the blueprint for a building—it defines how visitors will enter and move around the site.

You can draw a Web site navigation diagram in a program like Adobe Illustrator or Microsoft Visio. But Dreamweaver allows you to generate site navigation while you create Web pages.

When you *prototype* site navigation, or sketch out a flowchart representing site links in Dreamweaver, you generate bare-bones pages that contain *only* links to other pages. The navigation bars that get generated are simple (**Figure 14a**).

> **Tip**
> *Once you prototype a site, you can save a graphical map of the links you create, and print or display that.*

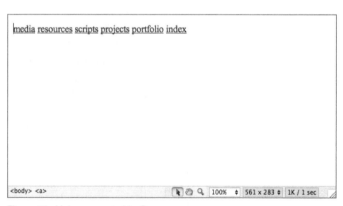

media resources scripts projects portfolio index

`<body> <a>`   100%   561 x 283   1K / 1 sec

Figure 14a Links generated by Dreamweaver.

To prototype a Web site, and in the process generate pages with links, display the Files panel (press the F8 function key if the Files panel is not visible). Then follow these steps:

1. From the Files panel menu, choose File > New File.

2. In the Files panel, rename the new file you created index.htm.

Index.htm or Index.html Is Your Home Page

Different servers have different rules for home pages, but generally the index.htm or index.html file serves as a Web site home page. The home page is the file that opens when a visitor comes to your site. This has more significance when your site is transferred to a remote server and made accessible to visitors. But even when you are only working with a local site, defining a home page is necessary to generate a site map or prototype navigation links using the Dreamweaver Files panel.

3. Control-click (Mac) or right-click (Windows) the file you created and named index.htm. From the context menu, choose Set As Home Page.

4. From the Files panel menu, choose View > Site Map. The home page appears as an icon (**Figure 14b**).

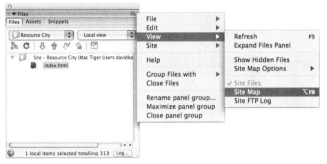

Figure 14b Defining a home page in Site Map view.

5. Expand the Files panel by clicking the Expand icon (**Figure 14c**).

Figure 14c Expanding the Files panel in Site Map view.

6. Choose File > New File from the Files panel menu. Create several new files, and assign filenames (with no special characters like $, ^, or #). Add an *htm* or *html* filename extension to each file.

7. Click the link icon next to the home page, and click and drag to create a connection to one of the files you created.

You can draw links from the home page to other pages, and from other pages to the home page. Or between any two pages. The page you draw a link *from* has a link placed on it to the page you draw a link *to*.

continued on next page

#14: Prototyping Site Navigation

8. Select any page icon and click and drag to another page icon to create links. As you do, a site map schematic appears in the Files panel (**Figure 14d**).

9. To see one of your pages with the generated link bar, double-click the page to open it in Page view.

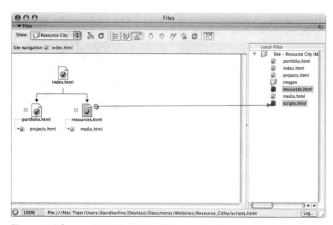

Figure 14d Generating links in the Files panel.

#15 Generating and Viewing Site Maps

As you draw links in Site Map view, you'll generate navigation links on the pages. These links are rather crude; they are simply a horizontal bar of text links. They work, but from a practical point of view, they are only bare-bones Web pages, and requiring further content and formatting before they are "real" Web pages with content and style.

The most valuable thing you create when you define links in the Site Map view is a prototype of site navigation links that can be saved as an image, shared with clients, and/or used as a guide to site development.

To save a site map as an image, follow these steps:

1. Click the Expand/Collapse icon to collapse the Files panel.

2. From the Files panel menu, choose View > Site Map Options > Layout to define site map display options (**Figure 15a**).

Figure 15a Defining site map display options.

The Site Definition dialog opens with the Site Map Layout category selected. You can control the number of columns that display and the width of the columns by entering values in the Number of Columns and Column Width boxes. The Number of Columns box defines the maximum number of pages that display per row. The Column Width box defines the width (in pixels) of site map columns. You can also choose to display either page filenames or more descriptive page titles. After formatting your site map, click OK.

continued on next page

Generating a Graphical Site Map

The technique described in this How-To can be used to create a graphical, clickable site map for your Web site. To do this, save the file, and then save the file as a GIF, PNG or JPEG file using a graphics image editor such as Photoshop or Photoshop Elements.

You can embed this image in a Web page and create clickable hotspots so that the site-map is an easy-to-follow, clickable navigation tool. Embedding images and defining clickable hotspots on images is explained in Chapter 9. "Embedding Images."

3. From the Files panel menu, choose select File > Save Site Map (**Figure 15b**).

Tip

You must click on the site map side of the divided Files panel to make the File > Save Site Map option active. It won't work if you have selected the right side of the expanded Files panel.

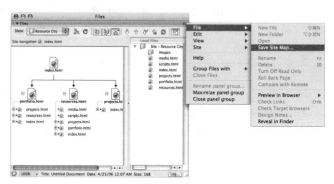

Figure 15b Saving a configured site map.

4. The Save dialog opens. Enter a filename and navigate to a folder (by default, the image is saved in your local site folder).

Note

The Windows version of Dreamweaver 8 allows you to save your file as either a BMP (Windows bitmap) or PNG (Web-compatible) file. If you're using a Mac, images are saved as PICT files. Any of these file formats can be opened, edited in Photoshop, and saved to any other image format.

5. After you define a filename and folder (and in Windows, choose a file format), click Save in the Save dialog.

CHAPTER FOUR

Connecting to a Remote Server

A *local* Web site is the folder on your computer where you create and save your site content. In order for others to access that content, you need to transfer those files to a *remote server*.

Normally, there are two versions of your Web site. The local site, on your computer, is where you create content. When that content is ready for the public, you upload it to the remote server.

In order for the remote (publicly accessible) site to match the content on your local site, all files must be transferred correctly, maintaining the same filenames and folder structure as exists on the local site. Dreamweaver provides the Files panel to manage your local site content, and you use the same Files panel to manage your *remote* site.

In this chapter, you'll learn how to define a remote server connection and transfer files back and forth between your local and remote sites.

You will also learn how to coordinate with other developers. Large Web design projects usually involve more than one designer or developer, with each person working at his or her local site as well as transferring files to and from the remote server. Dreamweaver 8 provides powerful tools to prevent multiple editors from working on the same page at the same time. Dreamweaver also includes tools for automating site management.

#16 Defining a Remote Server Connection

Can You Have a Remote Server with No Local Site?

It is *possible*—though generally not a good idea—to work on *just* a remote server. In this case, as soon as page content is edited and saved, it appears immediately on the remote server. There are two major dangers to this "remote-only" approach: There is no backup of your content if your server crashes. And there is no buffer between saving content on a page and making it available to the world; there's no chance to review, check, test, or supervise content before it becomes public.

In short, any site content worth developing is worth first developing on a local site, and then transferring to a remote site.

Normally, a remote server reflects content developed on a local site. In other words, most developers first create and test their Web pages on their own computer and then upload that content to a remote server once it has been tested, proofread, vetted and approved, and deemed ready to share.

The steps in this How-To assume you have already created a local Web site. If you have not, jump back to Chapter 3, "Defining a Web Site."

When you launch Dreamweaver, the site you had open at the end of your last session will open. Your open site is indicated in the Files panel, but if that panel is not displayed, there is nothing that indicates which site is open. To determine which site is open, choose Site > Manage Sites. The Manage Sites dialog opens, and the current open site is highlighted (**Figure 16a**).

Figure 16a Identifying the open site in the Manage Sites dialog.

With a site selected in the Manage Sites dialog, click Edit to open the Site Definition dialog. In the Site Definition dialog, choose the Advanced tab.

Tip
Both the Basic and Advanced tabs provide access to the tools necessary to define a remote server connection, but the Basic tab marches you through multiple wizard-type screens, while the Advanced tab provides easier access to and an overview of your connection options.

In the Advanced tab of the Site Definition dialog, click the Remote Info category. Then, follow these steps to define your remote server (**Figure 16b**):

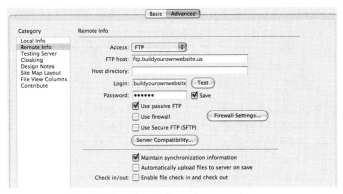

Figure 16b Defining FTP location, login, and password.

1. From the Access drop-down menu, choose FTP to define a connection to a remote server, or Local/Network if the remote site will be on another computer on your internal network.

2. In the FTP host field, enter the FTP location provided by your Web host provider.

3. In the Host directory field, enter the server folder information provided by your Web hosting company, if needed.

4. If your Web hosting company requires a host directory, enter the information they provided in the Host directory field.

5. In the Login field, enter the login or user name provided by your Web host provider.

6. In the Password field, enter the password provided by your Web host provider.

Signing up for a Remote Server

Shopping for a Web host can be simple if you are creating a small site with small files and not expecting a lot of traffic. Yahoo, for instance, offers a deal for about five dollars a month, and often throws in a free domain name (the name people type in their Web browser to get to your site—like davidkarlins.com).

If you plan to include large files (like video) or expect a lot of visitors (over 100 a day), or both, you'll want to do some comparison shopping before choosing a Web host. The site www.buildyourownWebsite. us has useful resources and articles for finding Web hosting and obtaining domain names.

After you pay for your remote server space, your Web host provider will give you three essential pieces of information: The FTP address, your login (user name), and your password. Some Web host providers also assign a host directory. If you didn't get that information, you can probably assume it is not necessary, but you might confirm with your site provider that there is no Host Directory.

Note

Password and login information is case-sensitive and must be entered exactly as provided. Once you have entered an FTP location, a login, and a password, you have defined the essentials of your connection.

7. If your Web host provider allows you to connect using passive FTP, select the Use passive FTP check box. You can try connecting to your site without this check box selected, and then try enabling passive FTP if your connection fails.

8. If you are working behind a firewall, your system administrator might need to configure the firewall settings in the Site Definition dialog. However, normally Dreamweaver adopts the same firewall settings you use with other programs to connect to the Internet, so custom settings are not necessary

9. After you define the remote connection, click the Test button. If your connection works, the confirmation dialog appears (**Figure 16c**).

Note

For now, ignore the three check boxes at the bottom of the dialog that define synchronized, automatic, and shared file management options. Those options are examined in #19, "Working with Other Developers," and #20, "Synchronizing Local and Remote Content."

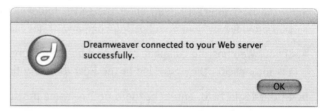

Dreamweaver connected to your Web server successfully.

OK

Figure 16c Connected!

#17 Connecting to a Remote Server

Simply defining a remote server connection does not automatically *connect* you to that server. When you open a Web site in Dreamweaver, you normally open only the local site.

Only after you actually *connect* to your remote site can you see what files are on that site and manage files at the remote server.

With a site open, you connect to your remote server by clicking the Connects to remote host button in the Files panel (in either expanded or collapsed view) (**Figure 17a**).

Figure 17a Connecting to a remote server via the Files panel.

Once you connect to a remote server, you can see either local or remote server content using the View pop-up menu in the Files panel (**Figure 17b**).

Figure 17b Viewing the content of the remote site.

Mirroring Local and Remote Sites

The Dreamweaver Files panel provides tools for managing files at both the local *and remote* servers. That is a potentially scary power to have. It means that you can rename, move, and delete files from your remote server and, in the process, corrupt your remote server files so they no longer match the files on your local server.

As a general rule, avoid editing filenames, folder locations, and so on at your remote server. In #18, you'll learn to transfer files from your local server to your remote server. If you stick to a protocol of creating and managing files on your local site, and then transferring those files to the remote site, you'll ensure that both sites match, and what you see on your local site will match what visitors see at your remote site.

To see the content of both the local and remote sites at the same time, click the Expand icon in the Files panel toolbar. In expanded mode, click the Site Files icon in the File panel toolbar (**Figure 17c**).

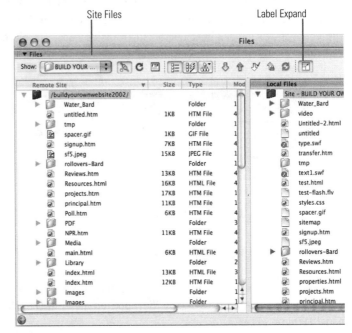

Figure 17c Comparing local and remote site content.

Note

If you choose Site Map view, you can't see the remote site. The third view option, Testing Server, displays connections to live data—a topic that is beyond the scope of this book. The topic is covered in excellent detail in Macromedia Dreamweaver 8 Advanced for Windows and Macintosh: Visual QuickPro Guide by Lucinda Dykes (Peachpit Press).

#18 Transferring Files

You can transfer files from the local site to the remote site, or vice versa, in the expanded Files panel. You can *upload* files to the remote site right in the Document window. And you can view both the local and remote sites in the collapsed Files panel.

Getting comfortable with transferring files in all three environments (Document window, expanded Files panel, and collapsed Files panel) allows you to conveniently and quickly transfer files and easily keep track of what is where.

There are two basic phases to transferring files to a remote server. The first phase is when you design and test the original site on your local computer, and then upload the whole site to your remote server. The second phase is when you edit elements of your site—first making changes to the local version, and then uploading only the changed parts of your site to the remote server.

To upload an entire site from your local folder to the remote server, click the root folder of your local site in the Files panel—either in expanded or collapsed view. With the root folder selected, click the Put Files icon in the Files panel toolbar (**Figure 18a**).

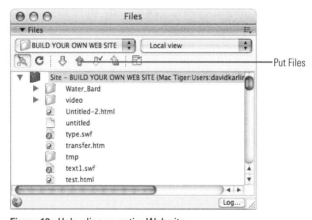

Put Files

Figure 18a Uploading an entire Web site.

Background File Transfer

Dreamweaver 8, for the first time, allows you to continue editing Web pages while files are transferred from local to remote sites (or from remote to local sites).

This is a huge relief for those of us who have twiddled our thumbs for hours, waiting for Dreamweaver to become functional only after file transfer was complete.

Although you can edit Web pages while files transfer to (or from) a remote server, you cannot do other file management activity on the server while files are in transit. This means, for example, that you cannot edit your site in the Site Definition dialog while you are transferring files. But you can open a Web page on your local site and edit it.

Dreamweaver will prompt you to confirm the action by clicking OK, and then will upload your entire Web site. The Background File Activity dialog will track the progress of uploading your site (**Figure 18b**).

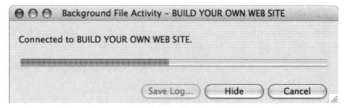

Figure 18b Transferring files in the background—you can continue editing pages in Dreamweaver while files transfer.

One you have uploaded your site, you won't want to waste time re-uploading the entire site each time you change a file. Instead, you can upload selected files. Use Shift-click or Command-click (Mac) or Ctrl-click (Windows) to select files in the Files panel, and choose Put to upload the selected files.

You can also upload open pages directly from the Document window. Do this by clicking the File Management tool in the Document toolbar and choosing Put (**Figure 18c**).

Figure 18c Uploading an open Web page.

In addition to putting (uploading) files to your server, you can also download files from your server. If you are working on a Web site by yourself (you are the only person who places files on the server in Dreamweaver), you will rarely need to transfer files from the remote server to your local computer, since all files originate on your local computer, and you can overwrite files on the server by uploading the matching file from your local computer. However, if you are working with other developers on a site, you might well need to download a file that was updated *by someone else*. In that case, click the file in the server, and click the Get Files button in the Files panel toolbar (**Figure 18d**).

Get Files

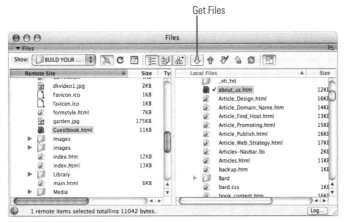

Figure 18d Downloading a file using the Get Files button in the Files panel.

#**19** Working with Other Developers

Automatic Check-Out

If you enable automatic check-in and check-out in the Remote Info category of the Site Definition dialog for your site, then every time you open a file, that file is automatically downloaded from the server and locked for editing at the server.

If two or more developers work on the same Web site, there is the danger that both will edit the same file on their local computers, at the same time. In that case, when they both upload their edited pages, the second page uploaded would overwrite the first, causing chaos, confusion, frustration, and disrupting the mellow harmonic vibes that should define the collaborative experience. You don't want that!

To prevent this, Dreamweaver provides a check-out feature that works like checking out a book at a library; only one developer can check out a page at a time.

Before multiple developers can use the check-out system in Dreamweaver, each developer has to enable this feature on his or her local computer. To do that, follow these steps:

To set up the Check In/Check Out system:

1. Chose Site > Manage Sites to open the Manage Sites dialog.

2. Your active site will be selected (if it is not, click it). Click Edit to open the Site Definition dialog. Select the Remote Info category.

3. Select the "Enable file check in and check out" check box. By default, the "Check out files when opening" check box is selected; keep it that way to automate the check-out process. Enter a name and e-mail address that will display when you check out a file. That way other developers will know who has checked out a page and is working on it, and can contact you if necessary (**Figure 19a**).

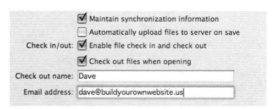

Figure 19a Enabling check-out, and providing contact information for other developers.

To check out a file, click the file in the Files panel, and click the Check Out icon in the Files panel toolbar. You will be prompted to download dependent files if necessary, and a dialog will ask you to approve overwriting the local version of the page. After you download the page, a check mark in the Files panel indicates that you have a file checked out. After you edit a file and save changes, use the Check In icon in the Files panel to upload the file back to the server and remove the checked-out status. Other developers can now access this file (**Figure 19b**).

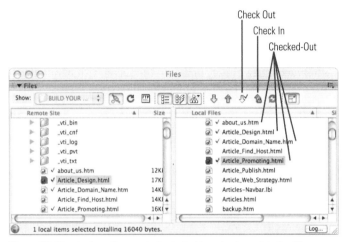

Figure 19b Checked-out files are indicated with a check mark in the Files panel.

#20 Synchronizing Local and Remote Content

If you are editing one or a few files at a time, you can fairly easily download (Get) the file, edit it, and then upload (Put) the file back to the server. Or on the other hand, if you are uploading an entire site, you can click the root folder in the local site, and click Put to upload the entire site.

What about in-between scenarios, when you have edited too many files to remember what has been updated, but you haven't done an entire site? If you upload only files you remember editing, you might neglect to upload important site content changes. If you play it safe and upload the entire site, you might end up transferring way more data than you need to, tying up Dreamweaver's site tools, and tying up and straining your Internet connection. Dreamweaver 8 introduces the Synchronize feature.

To synchronize files by updating the server with newer files from the currently open local site, follow these steps:

1. If you want to manually select files to synchronize, Shift-click or Command-click (Mac) or Ctrl-click (Windows) to select those files. Otherwise, by default, Dreamweaver will automatically detect changed files.

2. In the Files panel, choose either Remote view or Local view, depending on which direction you want to transfer files. Select Local view to transfer files to the remote server, and select Remote view to transfer files from the remote server to the local computer (**Figure 20a**).

Just Checking?

Dreamweaver provides tools to synchronize your local and remote site content rationally. If you are not ready to synchronize your site, but simply want to know which files on the local site are newer than those on the remote site, then click the Files panel menu and choose Edit > Select Newer Local. Newer files on the local site will be selected—both marked (highlighted) and selected for file management. They can be easily uploaded (Put) to the server.

To identify files on your remote server that are newer than those on your local computer (that is, files that have been edited on another computer, or by another developer since you downloaded them), click the Files panel menu and choose Edit > Select Newer Remote. Newer files on the server will be selected and can be easily downloaded.

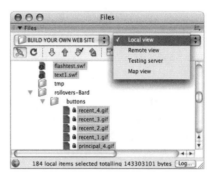

Figure 20a
Choosing Local view in the Files panel.

3. From the Files panel menu, choose Site > Synchronize. The Synchronize Files dialog appears. From the Synchronize pop-up menu in the Synchronize Files dialog, choose either selected files or the whole site.

4. In the Direction pop-up menu, choose from the options—get from server, put to server, or both—that allow you to transfer files from local site to server, server to local site, or both ways, replacing older files with more recent ones.

5. In the Synchronize Files dialog, click the Preview button. Dreamweaver connects to your remote site and creates a list of files that meet your criteria (new at the remote site, newer at the local site, or both). The list is displayed in a dialog (again) called Synchronize. Click OK, and Dreamweaver will update all files according to the criteria you defined (**Figure 20b**).

Figure 20b Synchronizing files.

CHAPTER FIVE

Creating Web Pages

Most of the content in your Web site will be inside a Web page. Some of this content, such as text, becomes part of your Web page file. Other content, such as images, is *embedded* in your Web page. Embedded objects appear in your Web page but are actually separate files. Content is positioned and laid out on Web pages either with tables or with CSS positioning objects.

Before diving into how to create Web pages and add content to them, it's helpful to separate appearance from essence in what makes up a Web page. When visitors view your page in a browser, they might see formatted text, images, and even a video. It *looks* to the visitor as if all of the elements are "part of" the Web page; however, some elements are part of the page and others (such as images and much of the formatting) are linked to or embedded in the page.

The reason for this quick overview of what is and what is *not* technically part of a Web page is to help put "creating a Web page" in perspective. Think of the Web page you create as a *container* for additional content. Or, to use a different metaphor, in many ways your Web page acts like a picture *frame,* providing a place for content.

Your Web page is the foundation on which to display all your content, such as images, media, and text. This makes it critical that you understand the basic components of a Web page and create them properly.

#21 Creating a New Page from Scratch

You can create a new Web page in Dreamweaver from either the Files panel or the Document window. Creating a new file in the Files panel simply generates an HTML page, while creating a new page in the Document window allows you to define the file type and automatically opens the file in the Document window for editing.

To create a new file from the Files panel, go to the Files Panel menu and choose File > New File (**Figure 21a**).

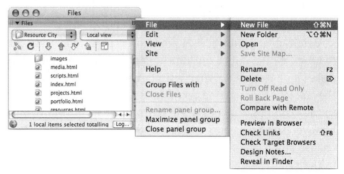

Figure 21a Generating a new file from the Files panel.

Files created from the Files panel menu are named untitled.html (or untitled2.htm, and so on). You can rename the file in the Files panel by choosing File > Rename from the Files panel menu, or by selecting the file in the Files panel and pressing the F2 function key.

The Files panel is a good place to work in if you're generating lots of new Web pages and plan to open and edit them later.

Most often, you'll create new files from the Document window. From the Document window menu, choose File > New. The New Document dialog opens. When you create files from scratch, that is, without using predefined templates, you'll need to select the General tab of the New Document dialog (**Figure 21b**).

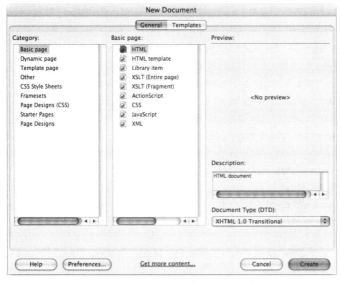

Figure 21b Defining a new file in the New Document dialog.

In the Category list, choose Basic page. In the Basic page list, choose HTML. In the Document Type (DTD) field, choose the default document type. Then click Create to generate a new Web page.

Once you create a new page, you need to *save* it, and you need to assign a page *title* to that page. Naming, saving, and assigning titles to pages is necessary whether you are creating a page from scratch or using a template or Starter or Design page. This is explained in #24, "Naming and Titling Pages."

Generating Pages in the Files Panel—a Scenario

When creating a large Web site, rather than working initially in the Document window to create one page at a time, many experienced designers start by generating all the files they plan to include in a Web site in the Files panel.

Later, after all pages have been generated, developers will open and edit the individual pages.

Another trick for quickly generating pages is to take one prototype page and copy it to create new pages. This, too, is best done in the Files panel. In the Files panel, select the page you want to copy, and choose Edit > Duplicate. The duplicate files will appear with filenames beginning with "Copy of... (the original filename)."

#22 Using Starter Pages and Page Designs

Starter Pages vs. Page Designs vs. Templates

Starter pages have generic content that can be adapted to various business sites. Design pages have page layouts, but no content (the content is filler type).

Templates work like Page Designs or Starter Pages except that you create them, and they include both editable and noneditable areas that cannot be changed unless you edit the source template. Templates and related tools for managing large sites are explored in Chapter 10, "Planning and Implementing Site Elements."

Starter Pages and Page Designs are underrated features in Dreamweaver 8. Starter pages are what would be called templates that provide fill-in-the-blanks pages that can be adapted to your business. Dreamweaver offers professionally designed, clean-looking pages for businesses in several categories, ranging from travel to personal training.

It's valuable to be familiar with the Starter Pages. They provide inspiration for your own page designs and content. You can start with a Starter Page (hence the name!) and edit the content to suit your needs, thus making the page unique.

Page Designs are even more valuable. You can learn page design aesthetics and techniques from studying them. In many cases, you can directly use predefined Page Designs as is for your site. For example, the Image: Slide Show Page Design creates a very usable image slide show page that can be used (and reused) for online slide shows. When you apply a unique style sheet to the page (CSS formatting is covered in Chapter 8, "Formatting Type"), the pages generated from the Starter Page will work fine as slide show pages in any Web site (**Figure 22a**).

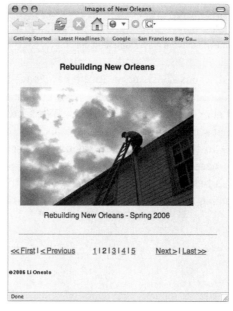

Figure 22a
A slide show page generated directly from a Starter Page, with a unique style sheet applied.

To create a page from a Starter Page, choose File > New. The New Document dialog opens. In the Category list, choose Starter Pages. In the Starter Pages list, you can choose different starter pages and examine the thumbnails to find a useful page. In the Description field of the dialog, you can find additional info on how to use the Starter Page (**Figure 22b**).

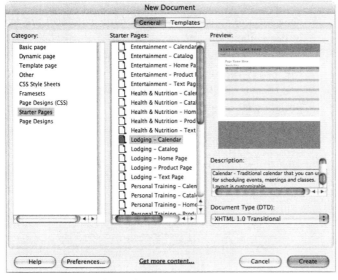

Figure 22b Examining Starter Pages.

After you choose an appropriate Starter Page, click Create to generate a new page. Then title and save the page using the steps in #24, "Naming and Titling Pages."

There are 30 available page designs. You can display them by choosing the Page Designs category in the New Document dialog. Each Page Design displays a Preview (thumbnail) and a description in the New Document dialog when you select it. Page Designs mostly fall into a few categories:

- Page Designs that start with Commerce are useful for designing e-commerce pages.

- Page Designs that start with Data can be adapted to present database content, such as catalog pages.

Why Not Use a Starter Page?

The obvious limitation of using a Starter Page is that sophisticated visitors might recognize that you've copied a Dreamweaver Starter Page. And it may well be the case that your content differs substantially from that on the Starter Page, in which case the "starter" content might not be of much help.

Never Mind the Topics... Use the Formatting

You'll quickly notice that Dreamweaver 8 comes with Starter Pages for several types of businesses, but all of these sets of Starter Pages include the same types of pages: Calendar, Catalog, Home Page, Product Page, and Text Page.

Regardless of your type of business, you'll most likely be able to adapt one of them to your needs.

#22: Using Starter Pages and Page Designs

Page Designs and Page Designs (CSS)

There are two basic techniques for designing Web pages: tables and CSS. Tables divide a page into (usually invisible) grids, into which you place content. Page design with tables is the most easy to learn and reliable technique for laying out Web pages, and is covered in Chapter 6, "Page Layout with Tables."

A more flexible and sophisticated method for designing pages is to define CSS objects that are positioned on a page using vertical and horizontal coordinates. Page design with CSS is explained in Chapter 7, "Page Layout with CSS Layers."

When you generate pages using preset Page Designs, you can choose Page Designs with tables or Page Designs (CSS) with style sheets.

Most people are better served using the basic Page Designs category. In this category, the tables are easier to work with and edit.

- Image Page designs include several approaches to designing pages that present images (including photos).

- The horizontal and vertical Master Page Designs are essentially template pages, with horizontal (or vertical) navigation areas.

- Text Page Designs offer page layouts suitable for long or short documents and articles.

- Page Designs that start with UI (*user interface*) are useful in designing forms, or pages to collect or display database content. To create a page from a preset Page Design, choose File > New. The New Document dialog opens. In the Category list, choose Page Designs. When you find an appropriate Page Design, click Create to generate a new page (**Figure 22c**).

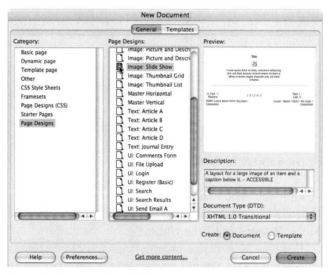

Figure 22c Choosing a Page Design.

After you generate a new page using a Page Design, create a title and save the page using the steps in #24, "Naming and Titling Pages."

#23 Choosing a Page Document Type

Regardless of how you generate a page—from scratch using a Page Design, or using a Starter Page—Dreamweaver provides many options for the Document Type Definition (DTD). The default document type in Dreamweaver is XHTML 1.0 Transitional. What does that mean? Why is it the default document type? And why should you accept that type when you create a document?

HTML (*hypertext markup language*) served the Web for years providing a modicum of formatting options. These formatting options became increasingly insufficient to meet the requirements of Web designers and visitors because HTML is too limited in its formatting tools. Also, it is not processed and displayed with much consistency in different browsers.

To address the shortcomings of HTML as a tool for flexible design and consistent display, the Web developer community has evolved more complex and reliable markup language standards that allow the current (and future) generations of browsers to display more page design features more consistently.

XHTML 1.0 Transitional is widely accepted as a safe and reliable document type. However, if your site administrator, supervisor, or consultant advises you to use another document type, you can go to the New Document dialog and choose that type in the Document Type (DTD) popup in the Description field.

Document Type Made Simple

You won't notice any substantial difference in Dreamweaver if you choose the default version of HTML (XHTML 1.0 Transitional) or another markup language standard. In making XHTML 1.0 Transitional the default format for saving pages, Dreamweaver is adhering to the most reliable format available for consistent Web page display in different browsing environments. In short, stick with the default XHTML 1.0 Transitional Document type.

Some developers prefer XHTML 1.0 strict (**Figure 23**). Developers focused on mobile devices sometimes prefer to use XHTML Mobile 1.0. An exploration of different document types and their advantages and disadvantages is beyond the scope of this book, but you can find additional information at www.w3.org.

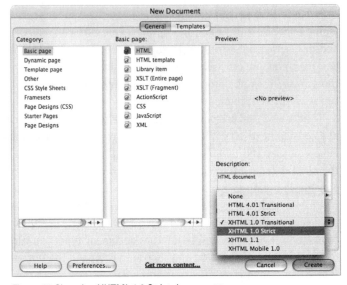

Figure 23 Choosing XHTML 1.0 Strict document type.

#24 Naming and Titling Pages

Every Web page needs a filename and a title. The filename is mainly an internal element. It is used to locate the file in a Web site and to link the file to other files. As such, filenames don't have to be very creative, but they should avoid special characters like commas, &, %, spaces and so on. You'll be safe if you stick to lower-case alphanumeric characters, plus the helpful dash and underscore characters.

There is a special requirement for filenames assigned to a site home page. A site home page is the page that opens when visitors enter your URL in the address bar of their browser. This URL does not specify a file, only a server location. Once the server location is open in a browser, browsers detect the home page by looking for a filenamed index.htm or index.html. Never create files named both index.htm and index.html; this will confuse your server, the browsers, and you. Instead, choose one or the other, and create a file called index.html (or index.htm). This will be your home page.

Note

Every Web site generally needs one index file. This file is named "index" and has a filename extension of either htm or html. You can create files with the same name but with different filename extensions (like index. htm and index.html, for example). But don't! Web browsers will recognize either htm or html as a Web page filename extension, but they will get confused if you have Web pages with the same name and different versions of the extension.

Pages titles are different from page filenames. Titles have nothing to do with how files are saved, linked to, or managed at a server. Therefore, they can contain any characters, including special characters like commas and other punctuation marks.

Page titles display in a browser title bar. Therefore, you should make them helpful and descriptive (**Figure 24a**).

Figure 24a A filename and page title displayed in a browser.

Other Home Page Options

There are other options for naming Web site home pages. Some servers require that you use default.htm or default. html instead of index.htm or index.html. Also, *active* server pages—pages with scripts that present data from a server database—use different filename extensions that correspond to the server script required to process data displayed on the page. These pages have filename extensions like .asp, .php, .csc, or .jsp. Active server pages are beyond the scope of this book.

Filenames are Server-Sensitive

Your operating system—be it Windows XP, Mac OS X, or something else—will probably have no trouble with filenames that include spaces and special characters, and will probably be able to handle uppercase and lowercase characters.

The tricky part is making sure your filenames are recognized and handled correctly by the operating system, file transfer system, and software on your *remote server* (the computer system that hosts your remote Web site). If you're wondering what operating system is being used, it's probably a version of Linux or Unix.

Ensuring compatibility with your Web host is why it's a good idea to follow the somewhat restrictive rules for naming Web page files in this technique.

When you save a page for the first time, you name the page by entering a filename. With a file open in the Save As dialog of the Document window, choose File > Save, and enter a filename in the Save As field (**Figure 24b**).

Figure 24b Saving and naming a Web page.

You can enter (or change) page title information in the Title field in the Document toolbar. If the Document toolbar is not visible in the Document window, choose View > Toolbars > Document (**Figure 24c**).

Figure 24c Entering a page title.

#**25** Defining Links and Link Attributes

Links are one of the most basic and dynamic elements of a Web page. In fact, hypertext, the "H" in HTML, refers to text that could have link properties (at least at the time the name was coined). Links can be associated with text or images.

> ### Note
> *In this technique, we'll focus on assigning links to text. In Chapter 9, "Embedding Images," you'll learn about some additional link features that apply only to images, like image maps, which are clickable parts of a picture.*

Links have three basic states: *unvisited, visited,* and *active.* Unvisited links display by default as underlined, blue type. Visited links—links that have been visited in a browser (before the browser cache was cleared)—display by default as underlined and purple. And active links—links to pages that are currently open—display in red.

> ### Note
> *You do not have to use default colors or attributes (like underlining) for styles. Also, you can define an additional link state (hovered) that displays when a link is rolled over by a mouse cursor. These changes to default link display are made with style sheets and are explained in Chapter 11, "Formatting Page Elements with CSS."*

You will *not* see link status in the Dreamweaver Document window. All links display in unvisited mode. This is because you haven't actually followed these links in Dreamweaver. You can only view links in visited or active states if you preview your page in a browser (choose File > Preview in Browser).

Generally speaking, link targets can be one of two types: internal to your site or outside your site. Links internal to your site are generally defined as relative links. That is, you don't define where the link is found on the Internet, you define where the link is located relative to the current page—and at your Web site.

When Do You See an Active Link?

Since active links become active when the linked page is open, they don't often display. Usually, when you click a link a page opens, but the page from which you linked to the new page closes (or is not visible because a new page has opened "on top" of it in a browser). There are, however, odd times when active links are visible. One of those times is when you design a page with frames. In that case, a linked page opens, but many browsers recognize the linking page as open as well—"framing" the linked page. Framed pages are discussed in Chapter 12, "Designing with Frames." You also see a link in the active state during the moment it takes for a page to open.

Absolute and Relative Links

You can define all links as absolute links—that is, define a full URL. The difference is that a link to your home page expressed as a relative link might simply be index.html, while the same link defined as an absolute link might be http://www.buildyourownwebsite.us/index.html.

Links, can be relative (within your site) or absolute (outside your site). Both are defined in the Property Inspector for selected text (or a selected image). To define an absolute link, start by selecting the text you want to link from. With the text selected, you can type an absolute link in the Link box in the Property Inspector (**Figure 25a**).

Link box

Figure 25a Entering an absolute link target for selected text.

To define a relative link, with the link text selected, click the blue Browse for File icon next to the link box in the Properties Inspector. The Select File dialog opens. Navigate to the linked file, and click Choose to generate a link to that file. The relative link appears in the Link box in the Property Inspector (**Figure 25b**).

Browse for File

Figure 25b Defining a relative link.

The other attribute that is important to define for a link is the Target window. By default, links open in the *same* browser window as the linking page, causing the linking page to disappear. A visitor can click the Back button on his or her browser to return to the original, linking page.

If you want a page to open in a *new* browser window, go to the Property Inspector and choose the _blank attribute in the Target popup menu (**Figure 25c**).

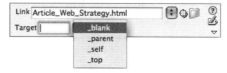

Figure 25c Defining the _blank link target that will open the link in a new browser window.

CHAPTER SIX

Page Layout with Tables

One great challenge for Web page design is that you have to design pages that work in different-size environments. They might be viewed on a large monitor displaying 1300 pixels or more in width or on a small handheld mobile device! Furthermore, different monitors and browsing environments display different resolutions. A 72-pixel–wide image might be 1 inch wide on one screen and $7/8$ inch wide on another. That eighth of an inch can be enough to ruin the alignment of a column or distort the display of a page.

Another constraint on Web page layout is a function of the evolution of HTML. In the early days of the Web, enterprising designers adapted tables to allow them to place objects (text, images, and now other objects including embedded media) inside table cells.

Although tables have been mostly replaced by CSS as the technique of choice for positioning page elements, especially as browser support for CSS has improved, tables remain a viable option for controlling page layout.

In an effort to provide a designer-friendly environment for page designers, Dreamweaver's Layout mode somewhat duplicates the kind of tools you find in programs like Illustrator, InDesign, or Photoshop. In Layout mode, you actually draw boxes on the page and place text, images, or other content in those boxes. As you draw these boxes, Dreamweaver actually generates a table with rows and columns that provide the table framework for the boxes you draw. Since Layout mode is really another way of defining tables, I strongly recommend that readers start with #26, " and then move on to Layout mode. That way, after you generate a table (invisibly) in Layout mode, you'll know what it is you have created.

#26 Creating a Table in Standard Mode

A basic, useful, and safe way to design a Web page is to first define a single-cell table, and then place page content inside that cell. Constraining page content in a rectangular table—especially constraining page *width* using a table—allows you to control the width at which your page displays in a browser. Creating a one-cell table is also a useful way of familiarizing yourself with the basic concepts involved in Web page design with tables.

To create a one-cell table for page content:

1. Open a new page (Choose File > New and select the Basic Page category and HTML in the New Document dialog; then click Create).

   With the new page open, your cursor is in the upper-left corner of the page by default. Insert a new table at the cursor by following these steps:

2. Choose Insert > Table from the Design window menu. The Table dialog appears.

   Tip
   Alternatively, you can click the Table button in the Layout panel of the Insert toolbar. See #6, "Using the Insert Toolbars," for an explanation of how to use the Insert toolbar.

3. In the Rows and Columns boxes, define the number of rows and columns in your table. It's easy to add rows and columns later, so when in doubt, simply generate a one-row, one-column table by entering 1 in both the Rows and Columns boxes.

4. In the Table Width box, enter a value representing either a number of pixels or a percentage of page width. Then, choose either pixels or percent from the Table Width popup menu (**Figure 26a**). For more on this, see #28, "Creating Fixed and Flexible Columns."

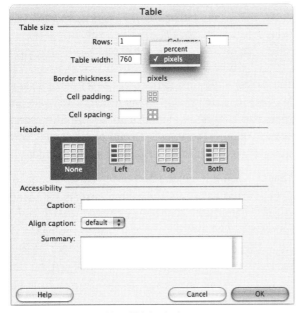

Figure 26a Defining table width in pixels.

5. The "Border thickness" box defines the width of the displayed border. Normally, tables used for page layout are defined with no border displayed. To display no border around a table, enter 0 (zero) in the Border Thickness box. Or, to display a border, enter a value such as 1 (for 1 pixel).

Tip

Table border color is defined in the Property inspector—see #30, "Defining Table Properties."

continued on next page

The One-Cell Table— A Foundation for Page Design

Even if your Web page doesn't require intricate design, you can constrain the display width of your Web page in a table. Placing content in a table enables you to define the width of your page in a browser. Without a table to constrain width (either to a fixed number of pixels or to a percentage of the browser window width), the page content will expand horizontally to fill the browser window. In many cases, that will make the text lines too long to be readable.

Experts differ over optimum page width, but the consensus is that a 760-pixel-wide table provides a convenient, accessible, and attractive framework for presenting text and images in a browser window.

Page *height* is normally not defined in a table. This is because if table width is fixed, the content has to have a direction in which it can expand if a viewer's browsing environment enlarges the content. This happens when a visitor's screen displays a lower resolution (causing images to expand on the screen), when type font size is increased, or for other reasons.

6. The "Cell padding" and "Cell spacing" boxes define the distance between cells and the padding inside a cell. Cell padding defines the buffer between cell content (like text or images) and the cell border. Cell spacing defines the spacing between cells.

Tip

A useful and often-used setting is to define 6 pixels of cell padding and 0 pixels of cell spacing. This prevents cell content from bumping into content in the adjoining cell, but at the same time eliminates the table "showing through" between cells, which is the point of defining cell spacing.

7. The Header and Accessibility areas of the Table dialog define features that are used by screen readers—software programs that read Web pages out loud to people who cannot read screen content. These tools are not particularly important or useful if you are using your table as a display tool.

They are useful if you are presenting large amounts of table data. In that case, left and/or top headers "announce" the nature of the content in the associated row (in the case of left headers) or column (in the case of top headers). Similarly, table captions and summaries are not necessary or helpful if you are using a table for page layout, but they can be helpful if you are presenting data that will be read out loud by reader software.

After you define a table in the Table dialog, click OK to generate the table. You will see the table displayed in the Document window even if you defined it with no border (**Figure 26b**).

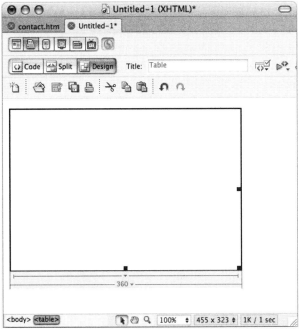

Figure 26b Viewing a table in the Document window.

#27 Creating a Table in Layout Mode

After you've worked with tables as a design tool for millennia, or at least a few months, you begin to "think in tables," and you can draw tables that provide boxes for content on the screen. But until you achieve that state of consciousness, and to provide a more comfortable table-drawing logic, Dreamweaver provides Layout mode.

Layout mode is a more intuitive way to draw boxes for page content, but Layout mode lacks features that define critical and basic properties of tables such as table alignment and border width. In short, you draw tables in Layout mode and then revert to Standard mode to enter content into your table and define features like table background or border color.

In Layout mode, you begin by electing to draw either a cell or a table, and then clicking and dragging the screen to create a table or cell anywhere on the page. If you elect to draw a cell and you haven't created a table yet, Dreamweaver handles that for you. If you draw a table, you can either draw cells inside that table or you can draw another (embedded) table within that table.

Note

Drawing a table inside a table increases the challenges and complexity of designing a page, and sometimes does so unnecessarily. Quite complex page designs can be achieved using a single table with many cells. There are times when a page design requires embedded tables. Techniques and challenges involved in embedding tables within tables are explained in #29, "Embedding Tables within Tables."

To draw a table in Layout mode, follow these steps:

1. Choose View > Table Mode > Layout Mode. As soon as you select Layout mode, the Insert bar displays (if it is not already displaying) with the Layout tools.

2. To draw a table, click the Layout Table button in the Insert bar. To draw a cell (and automatically generate a table if necessary), click the Draw Layout Cell button in the Insert bar (**Figure 27a**).

Figure 27a The Insert bar in Layout mode.

3. Click and drag to define the table height and width. Or, a simpler, easier technique is to click the Draw Layout Cell button in the Insert bar and draw a cell on the page. A table is generated to define the cell (**Figure 27b**).

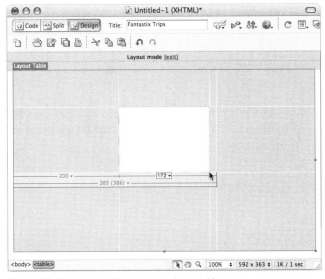

Figure 27b Drawing a cell and generating a table.

continued on next page

#27: Creating a Table in Layout Mode

Define in Layout Mode, But Edit in Standard Mode

Layout mode provides access to useful tools for defining table and cell properties. But when you select a cell in Layout mode, the Property inspector does not provide easy access to tools for formatting the content of the cell. On the other hand, in Standard mode, the Property inspector allows you to format either

4. After you define a table (by drawing either a table or a first cell), you can draw additional cells within the table. As you do, the table grid can become quite complex. You can also select a cell you already generated, and click and drag on a side or corner handle to change the height or width of that cell (**Figure 27c**).

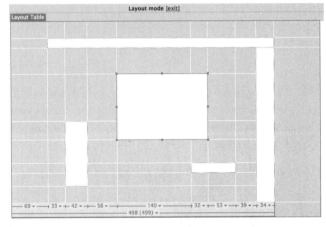

Figure 27c Generating a complex table by defining and editing many cells.

5. After you define your table structure, click the [exit] link at the top of the table to get out of Layout mode and into Standard mode.

#28 Creating Fixed and Flexible Columns

A widely used and very functional technique for page design involves creating tables that combine fixed columns with a flexible column. Very frequently, Web pages are built around tables that have a locked (fixed-width) left and right columns and a center column that expands to fill a specified percent of a browser window.

For example, a table might provide a 100-pixel–wide column on the left side of the page for navigation, a 100-pixel–wide column on the right, and a flexible column that fills all the remaining available space in a browser window (**Figure 28a**).

Fixed column width remains the same regardless of size of browser window

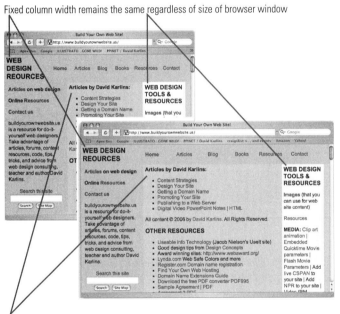

Flexible column width expands depending on size of browser window

Figure 28a Fixed and flexible columns.

The steps below can be used to create a Web page with two fixed-width columns and one flexible-width column. To apply these steps, choose Standard mode (either by clicking on the Standard button in the Insert bar or by choosing View > Table Mode > Standard Mode).

1. Create a new three-column table by choosing Insert > Table. In the Table dialog, enter 3 in the Columns box, and enter 1 in the Rows box.

2. Set Table Width to 100%.

3. Set Border thickness to 0, Cell padding to 6, and Cell spacing to 0. Click OK to generate a three-column table that will fill 100% of a browser window (**Figure 28b**).

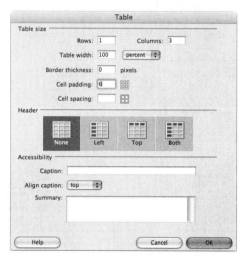

Figure 28b
Defining a three-column table that fills 100% of a browser window.

4. Select the left column in the table by clicking in it or on top of it, and enter 100 in the W (Width) box in the Property inspector (**Figure 28c**).

Tip

Column width is one of the properties of a table explained in more detail in #30, "Defining Table Properties." As explained there, height and width are usually defined in pixels, which is the default setting in the Property inspector.

Figure 28c Setting column width to 100 pixels.

Tip

If the Property inspector is not visible, press Ctrl (Windows) or Command (Mac) + F3.

5. Set the column width for the right column to 100 pixels.

Tip

By default, columns that are not defined as autostretch have a fixed, or locking width. Locking column widths only ensures that the width of the column does not get smaller than the set amount of pixels. If you place a large image in a column, the column will expand to accommodate the width of that image.

6. Switch to Layout mode by clicking the Layout Mode button in the Insert bar, or by choosing View > Table Mode > Layout Mode. Layout mode has the advantage of allowing you to easily define a column as autostretch—a feature that is harder to access in Standard mode.

7. Click the triangle icon at the bottom of the middle column, and from the popup menu choose Make Column Autostretch (**Figure 28d**).

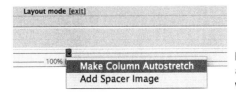

Figure 28d Defining a flexible column width.

You can now add content to the columns you defined. When the page is viewed in a browser, the middle column will expand or contract horizontally when the width of the browser window is changed.

Spacer Images

Dreamweaver locks the widths of the non-autostretch columns by inserting a repeating image with no visible height to prevent browsers from adjusting the width of these locked columns. This very small image is called a *spacer image*, and the first time such an image is inserted Dreamweaver generates one by default and names it spacer. gif. The first time you do this, you will be prompted to create a spacer image file. Dreamweaver will generate and name that file. Or if you already have a spacer file, Dreamweaver will prompt you to use it. If, in fact, you already had Dreamweaver generate a spacer.gif file, you can either use it, or replace it by generating an identical one.

#29 Embedding Tables within Tables

Many page designs can be created by dividing a table into rows and columns. More complex page layouts might require embedding tables inside other tables. One reason for this is that there are properties of a table that apply to *all* cells in a table—specifically cell spacing and padding. And there may be times when you need to combine page elements enclosed in a table with no buffer (a banner on the top of a page is an example of this), with page elements that are in columns buffered with spacing between cells.

In the scenario above, a clean way to design the page would be to create one "master" table with no cell spacing or cell padding. At the top of the table, you could embed one, one-column table with no cell padding or spacing. Under that, you could embed a second table with three columns, and content separated by 6 pixels of cell spacing (**Figure 29a**).

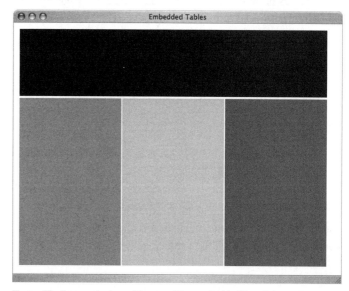

Figure 29a A page design with two tables embedded in a "master" table.

There are a couple tricks involved in embedding a table within a table. The following steps will walk you through the process safe and sound:

Expanded Tables Mode

When you have trouble selecting a table, or cells within a table, try using Expanded Tables mode. This display mode creates thicker borders around your table and the cells within it.

The expanded border around the table, which is easier to see and select, does not actually appear when the table is viewed in a browser. Expanded Tables mode simply helps you identify and select the table in the Document window.

1. Create the first table with one column, one row, no border, no cell spacing, and no cell padding. See #26, "Creating a Table in Standard Mode," for details. Set the width of the table with a value in pixels or percent. This value will set the outside limits of the page width, and all tables you embed within your table will be no wider than the width you define here. Click OK to generate the table (**Figure 29b**). The table appears in the browser window.

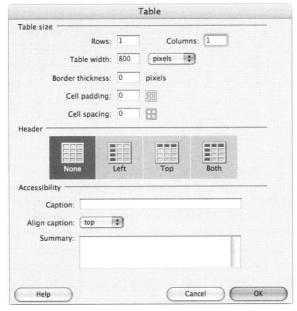

Figure 29b Defining a "master" table in which other tables will be embedded.

2. In order to see the table and table elements clearly as you embed tables within it, choose Expanded table view. Do this by clicking the Expanded button in the Insert bar, or by choosing View > Table Mode > Expanded Tables Mode. A more easily visible and selectable border appears around the single-cell table.

continued on next page

#29: Embedding Tables within Tables

Embedded Table Widths

Setting the width of an embedded table at 100% causes the table to fill the width of the table in which it is embedded, not 100% of the browser window. This setting is helpful if you want to make sure that any other embedded tables placed inside the "master" table stay below the first one.

3. As you insert tables within the table, you are actually inserting them within that table's single *cell*. Vertical alignment in tables is defined by cell. Click in the cell and choose Top in the Vertical field in the Property inspector (**Figure 29c**).

Tip

Different cells in a table can have different vertical alignments. Oddly enough, the default vertical alignment setting for cells is middle—so content drops to the middle of the cell as you enter it. Here you want the vertical cell alignment set to Top so that content fills columns from the top.

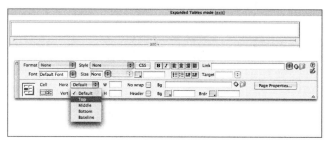

Figure 29c Setting vertical alignment to Top.

4. With your cursor still in the single cell of the table, choose Insert > Table. Now you can define any table properties you wish—choose a number of columns and rows, define borders, and cell padding or spacing. The only trick is that if you want your embedded table to fill the table in which it is placed, you need to set the width to 100%.

5. Select the embedded table by clicking the embedded table border. Press the right arrow key on your keyboard to place the insertion point just to the right of the embedded table. Choose Insert > Table to place a new table and define table properties. Here, again, you will probably want to set the width of the second embedded table at 100% (**Figure 29d**).

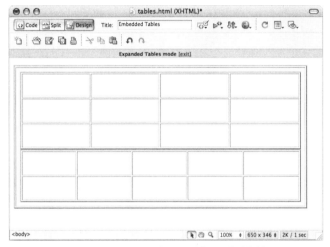

Figure 29d Two embedded tables viewed in Expanded Tables mode to make them easier to see and select.

#**30** Defining Table Properties

Table properties include elements like height, width, cell spacing, cell padding, border width and color, and background color or image. All these features can be defined in the Property inspector.

The trick is to select a *table* and not a cell. With the table selected, the Property inspector (**Figure 30**) allows you to define table properties, and with a cell selected you can define cell properties (see #31, "Defining Cell Properties," for details).

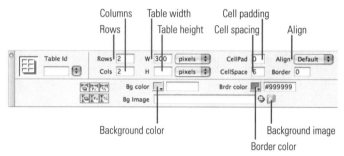

Figure 30: The Property inspector with a table selected.

Some table features are rather esoteric. Table ID is used when the table is controlled by scripts (like a JavaScript animation). The Class pop-up menu is used to apply CSS styles to the table.

Note
CSS formatting is covered in Chapter 11, "Formatting Page Elements with CSS."

Other features in the Property inspector are shortcuts for things like converting values from pixels to percent or vice versa—operations that don't normally require programmed interactivity because they really aren't that useful as design techniques.

The critical options in the Property inspector are:

- The Rows and Cols boxes define (or change) how many rows or columns are in a table. Adding to the existing number adds a row below the bottom row, or a column to the right of the last existing column. Lowering the value deletes rows or columns starting from the right or bottom of the table.

- Table Width (W) and Height (H) can be defined in pixels or percent. Normally, table height is not defined, as it will vary depending on the amount of content in the table.

- CelPad defines space (in pixels) between the border of a cell and cell content. CellSpace defines space (in pixels) between cells.

- The Align options pull-down menu places the table on the left (default), right, or center of the page.

- Bg color defines background color; a color selection palette appears when you click the box.

- Brdr color defines the color of a border if border width is set to a value greater than zero.

- Bg image defines a tiling (repeating) image that fills the background of the table.

Unnatural Selection of Tables and Cells

To define table properties, you must select a *table* and *not any cell* in that table. Expanded Table mode makes it easier to identify and click on a table border. Other tricks include using the Tag bar on the left side of the Status bar to click a <table> tag.

Alternatively, if you have a cell selected in a table, you can choose Edit > Select Parent Tag from the menu repeatedly until your table is selected.

#31 Defining Cell Properties

The cell Property inspector appears when a cell is selected in a table. Normally, selecting a cell is easier than selecting a table and doesn't present the same confusing challenge. Unless you click the table border, when you click inside a table, you select a table cell.

Some cell properties duplicate table properties. Background color can be defined for a cell or for a table. Border color and cell background images can also be defined for both tables and cells. Other cell properties cannot be defined for a table. Vertical alignment can only be defined for cells. The Property inspector also allows you to merge selected cells or split a cell.

The Property inspector that appears for a selected cell displays formatting options for type (or other selected objects, like an image) in the top section. In the bottom section, you define cell properties (**Figure 31a**).

Tip
If you can't see the bottom section of the Property inspector, click the Expand (down-pointing) triangle in the lower-right corner of the Property inspector.

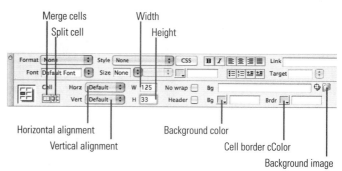

Figure 31a The Property inspector for a selected cell or cells.

To set a cell width, enter a value in the Width box. To set cell height, enter a value in the Height box. You can also adjust cell height and width by simply clicking and dragging the divider between cell rows or columns. (**Figure 31b**).

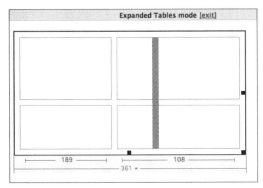

Figure 31b Changing column width by dragging the divider between columns.

To combine cells, click and drag to select contiguous (touching) cells, and click the Merge Cells button in the Property inspector. To split a cell, select the cell and click the Split Cell button in the Property inspector. The Split Cell dialog appears, allowing you to define how cells are split (**Figure 31c**).

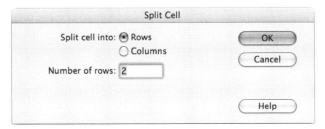

Figure 31c Splitting cells.

Page Layout with Layers and CSS

As I explained in Chapter 6, "Page Layout with Tables," the technique of using tables for page design is reliable; it is supported in nearly every browsing environment, and, in a way, it is easy. With Dreamweaver, the process of designing pages with tables is—or at least can be—quite simple.

As page design has become more important in the browsing experience, *style sheets*—essentially additional formatting options—were developed and became widely supported as a way to both format page elements (like text) and also define page layout itself.

Since this chapter introduces Cascading Style Sheets (CSS) as a design tool, I will briefly explain CSS. "Cascading" refers to the fact that styles are applied to page elements, pages, and sites using a a hierarchy. A *local style*, which applies to just one page, or even to just selected text, overrides all other styles that might be applied. If no local style exists, then the next most specific style is applied, and so on, up through a set of styles that ultimately are applied sitewide. Sitewide styles usually reside in *external style sheets:* documents that are separate from your Web pages but referenced by them for style information.

Page Design with CSS

In this chapter, we will use only local CSS formatting. External style sheets, which can be used to set up styles for any or all pages in your site, are addressed in Chapter 11, "Formatting Page Elements with CSS."

Should you use tables or CSS for page design? Tables are simpler to learn and you can feel more confident that your pages will look the way you intend in most desktop browsers. On the other hand, current thought on Web site construction is that using CSS makes your content easier to distribute on different platforms and can help you make it accessible to users with disabilities. In Dreamweaver, working with CSS is more like designing in Illustrator, Photoshop, or InDesign; and less predictable in its display in a wide range of browsing devices.

There is one more downside to using CSS for page design in Dreamweaver. While Dreamweaver makes it seamless, intuitive, and easy to apply CSS for text formatting, this cannot be said for page-level design. You can do it, but Dreamweaver doesn't give you the same ability to generate page layout CSS as you would have if you hand-coded the CSS. That said, you can create a professional-looking Web page with Dreamweaver's CSS page-design tools.

Dreamweaver provides two approaches to page design with CSS: Layers and Divs. Layers are a feature of Dreamweaver, not a part of XHTML or CSS, but they are easy to use, particularly if you've worked with layers in a program like Photoshop. Divs are part of the XHTML spec; in Dreamweaver they are less intuitive than layers to work with, but they provide more control over page design.

#32 Creating and Placing Layers

Layers are boxes on a Web page that hold content such as type, images, or other objects like media. Layers are defined both by their location on a page and their size (measured in pixels). As you will see later in this chapter, layers are more flexible than tables, and you can define more properties for layers than are available for tables.

Dreamweaver allows you to simply draw layers on the page, just as if you were designing in a program like Illustrator, Photoshop, or InDesign. As you draw, resize, or move a layer, Dreamweaver generates CSS that defines the location and size of that layer.

To draw a layer in an open document, choose Insert > Layout Object > Layer. A layer appears in the document. By default, this layer is 200 pixels by 115 pixels and is located at the top-left edge of your page (**Figure 32a**).

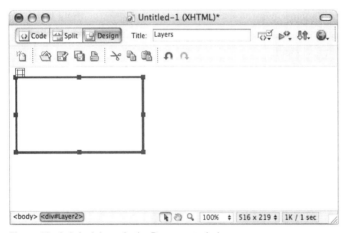

Figure 32a A default layer in the Document window.

When you generate a layer, it is selected, and you can edit it. If you deselect the layer by clicking elsewhere on the page, you can reselect it by clicking on the layer border.

You can move or relocate a layer in the Document window. To move a layer, click the layer handle (the icon in the upper-left corner of the selected layer), and simply drag it to another part of the page (**Figure 32b**).

Overlapping Layers

Technically, you *can* create overlapping layers. You might be able to produce some cutting-edge page designs this way and come close to simulating the freedom you have in programs like Illustrator, Photoshop, or InDesign to stack objects on top of each other.

If you do overlap layers, you can assign Z-index values to selected layers in the Property inspector, which defines the layers' "front-to-back" properties. Higher Z-index value layers display *on top of* lower Z-index value layers.

Overlapping layers are not universally supported in different browsing environments. They are less reliable than layers in general. And, unless you are pretty expert at CSS, there are a number of pitfalls in designing with overlapping layers that can sink your Web page, including the fact that layers often expand in size in different browsing environments in a way that can turn your page into gibberish if overlapping layers are used.

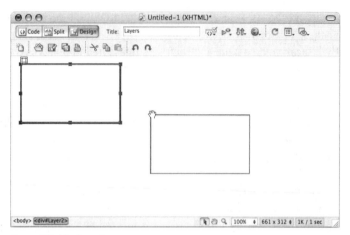

Figure 32b Moving a layer.

Dreamweaver offers tools to resize or align multiple layers. First, Shift-click to select all the layers you want to resize or align. Then, choose Modify > Arrange. From the submenu, you can select an alignment option (Align Left, Align Right, Align Top, or Align Bottom), or you can select Make Same Width or Make Same Height (**Figure 32c**).

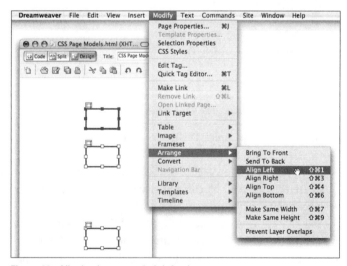

Figure 32c Aligning layers on their left edges.

Note

If you use the Modify menu to make selected layers the same height or width, the larger layer(s) will change size to match the smaller/smallest layer.

Display support for layers in the Dreamweaver document window has to be described as unpredictable. In my version of Dreamweaver 8, layer backgrounds sometimes do not display correctly. To reliably see how layers will look in a particular browser, you need to preview your page in that browser (**Figure 32d**). To do this from Dreamweaver, choose File > Preview in Browser. If you have more than one installed browser, select the desired browser from the submenu. Then you will see the page (and your layers) as viewers with that browser will see it.

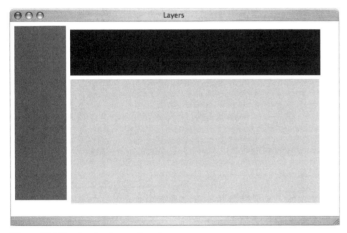

Figure 32d Previewing layers in a browser.

You can also embed a layer within another layer. This is somewhat analogous to embedding a table inside a table. The embedded layer is positioned *within* the layer in which it is placed. To embed a layer within a layer, click inside one layer and then insert another layer. Placing a layer within a layer can create unnecessarily complex pages that are difficult to edit. If your CSS page designs are too complex for layers, consider invoking definable Div tags.

Tip

Div tags are explored in #35, "Creating Divs."

#32: Creating and Placing Layers

#33 Formatting Layers in the Property Inspector

Layer Properties Are Not Universally Supported

The formatting attributes that you can assign to a layer are not supported in all browsing environments. Features like background color, background image, and overflow are particularly unpredictable.

As a general rule, if you want your site to be widely accessible in many browsing environments, use layers to *place* page content, but avoid relying on layer formatting features.

Not all layer formatting features are displayed in the default Document window settings. To view layer backgrounds, choose View > Visual Aids > CSS Layer Backgrounds.

You can move and resize layers using the Property inspector. Defining location and size in the Property inspector is more precise than clicking and dragging with a mouse because you can define exact location, height, and width to the pixel.

To define a location on a page in the Property inspector for a selected layer, enter a distance from the left edge of the page (in pixels) in the L field, and enter a distance from the top of the page in the T field. A layer with L and T values of zero will be placed in the upper-left corner of the page (**Figure 33a**).

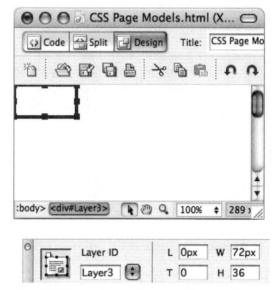

Figure 33a Placing a layer in the upper-left corner of a page.

The other definable elements of layers are (**Figure 33b**):

Clip   Vis   Bg image

Overflow   Z-index   Bg color

Layer ID   Class

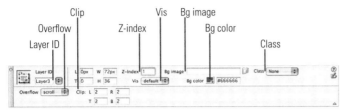

Figure 33b Defining layer properties.

- Layer ID: Defines the layer for use in scripts (the Layer ID must contain only alphanumeric characters—no spaces—and start with a letter).

- Overflow: Defines how content that is larger than the layer will appear in a browser. By default, layers stretch to fit content.

- Clip: Allows a specified amount of content in a layer to be "covered up" on the Left (L), Top (T), Right (R), or Bottom (B).

- Z-index: A numerical value for the bottom-to-top order of a layer that overlaps others. Higher-value layers appear on top of lower-value layers.

- Vis: Defines visibility—normally layer content is visible, but layers used in scripts are sometimes hidden to later be made visible by actions of a visitor.

- Bg image: Defines the image that appears as a background in the layer.

- Bg color: Defines the background color for a layer. If you defined a Bg image, the image will override a background color.

- Class: Applies style using a CSS class (see Chapter 11, "Formatting Page Elements with CSS" for an explanation of how to define CSS classes).

#34 Managing Layer Properties in the Layers Panel

The Layers panel is valuable when you are designing a page with layers. You can easily select layers in the Layers panel (even if you have set the layers' visibility) and make them visible in the Document window.

The Layers panel also provides a different and sometimes easier way to define layer visibility and Z-index values than using the Property inspector. For one thing, you can see the properties of many layers at a time in the Layers panel, which comes in handy when you are designing complex interactive pages with layers that are either hidden or visible depending on the state of a script that governs their properties.

You can also rename layers in the Layers panel, but remember, layer names must be alphanumeric and cannot start with a number.

View the Layers panel by choosing Window > Layers. The panel appears with all existing layers listed (**Figure 34a**).

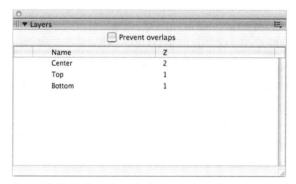

Figure 34a Selecting a layer in the Layers panel.

You select a layer in the Document window by clicking it in the Layers panel. To rename a layer in the Layers panel, double-click the layer name and enter a new name. You can also switch among the three visibility states in the Layers panel by clicking in the visibility column on the left. The closed eye icon means the layer is hidden. The open eye icon means the layer is visible. No icon signifies default status, which generally means the layer is visible unless a browser setting conflicts with it (**Figure 34b**).

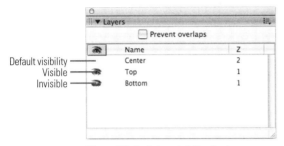

Default visibility
Visible
Invisible

Figure 34b Defining visibility for layers.

#35 Creating Divs

Dreamweaver layers allow designers to lay out pages using familiar tools, and the resulting code is CSS. But Dreamweaver 8 also lets designers work directly with CSS code, which is more powerful but also more complex. Designers can control page geography in CSS with the Div tag. Divs are essentially page sections (or containers) that can be defined with any set of attributes supported by CSS.

With Divs you can define many more attributes than with layers. Like layers, they can be positioned at absolute locations on a page, but they can also be positioned *relative* to other locations on a page. Also, like layers, Divs can be sized, but you can also define spacing between them or padding within them, as you can with table cells.

In fact, you can apply an almost unlimited number of attribute combinations to Divs, including border color, thickness, and type.

Note

For a fuller exploration of CSS formatting for objects like tables or page backgrounds, *see Chapter 11, "Formatting Page Objects with CSS."*

In Dreamweaver, there are almost as many ways to generate and define a Div as there are possible attributes. The following set of steps provides a digestible approach that I use to teach students how to create Divs.

To create a Div and specify its position:

1. In a new document, select Insert > Layout Objects > Div Tag. The Insert Div Tag dialog appears.

   The Insert Div Tag dialog itself does not help much with defining the positioning, size, or other attributes of the Div you want to create. But it does allow you to name it.

2. In the ID field of the Insert Div Tag dialog (**Figure 35a**), enter an alphanumeric name (start with a letter; spaces are allowed). Pick a name that will help you remember what this object is in case you create many Divs.

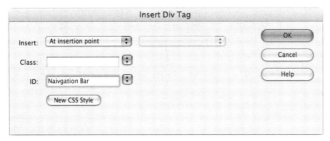

Figure 35a Naming a Div.

3. Do not click OK yet. All you've done so far is establish an invisible, contentless, sizeless section on your page. Instead, click the New CSS Style button in the Insert Div Tag dialog. The New CSS Rule dialog opens. In the next set of steps, you will define CSS rules that apply to the Div you created.

4. In the New CSS Rule dialog, leave the Selector Type radio button selection at Class, which is the default. Classes are highly flexible and can be applied to any element (including your Div). Select the "This document only" radio button. Then, in the Name field, enter a name (alphanumeric only) for the style. Then click OK (**Figure 35b**).

The CSS Rule Definition dialog opens when you click OK in the New CSS Rule dialog. Here is where you set up the class attributes that will be applied to your new Div.

continued on next page

What's with the Period in the Style Name?

Classes begin with a period. You don't need to enter the period when you name the style; Dreamweaver inserts it for you. The periods in class names denote that these styles are *appended to* other styles. For example, in Chapter 11 you will learn to define styles for both heading text and body (regular) text. However, you can append (attach) a *class* style to *either* or *both* of these tags.

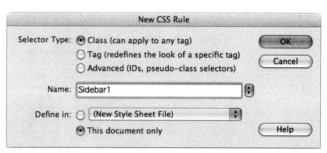

Figure 35b: Creating a class with style attributes that will apply to a Div.

Note

If you select the top "Define in" radio button instead of the "This document only" button, you must create a new, external style sheet file. External style sheets are explained in Chapter 11, "Formatting Page Elements with CSS."

5. In the CSS Rule Definition dialog, click the Positioning category. Here, you will choose which type of positioning to use when specifying the location of your Div, define the Div's size, and then define its location on or relative to other parts of the page (**Figure 35c**).

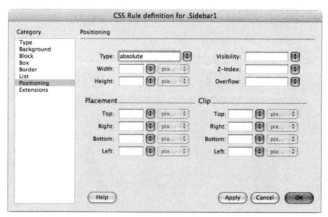

Figure 35c Defining the rules for the .Sidebar1 class, which will determine the positioning of a Div.

6. From the Type pop-up menu, first choose a positioning type.

- Choosing Absolute places the object at specific values from the upper-left corner of the page.

- Fixed freezes the object on a page so that when a visitor scrolls up or down, the object stays in the same place.

- Relative places the object relative to its position in the text flow of the page. If your cursor is at the top of a Web page, absolute and relative positioning have the same effect, but if your cursor is in the middle of some text, relative positioning places the object a defined distance to the left of and below the current cursor point.

- Static places the layer at its location in the text flow.

8. Define the width and height of your Div in the Width and Height fields. Choose a unit of measurement from the pop-up menu next to each box (pixels are normally used for defining dimensions in Web design, and using pixels is the most reliable way to size objects).

9. Define the position of your box in the Placement area. You can define location in pixels (or other units) either from the top or bottom of the page and either from the left or right edge of the page.

10. The four Clip boxes work like masking in illustration programs. Clipping hides part of the outside of the content of a CSS positioning object.

11. Visibility defines whether or not the Div is visible.

12. The Z-index box defines how the Div will move in front of or behind other objects. Positioning objects with higher Z-index values appear on top of objects with lower Z-index values. If your positioning objects do not overlap, Z-index values are irrelevant.

continued on next page

13. The Overflow pop-up menu defines how text that does not fit in the positioning object will appear in a browser.

14. Once you have defined the options in the Positioning category, you have defined the basic location and size of your object (Div). Use the Border category to apply borders to your object. Use the Box category to define buffer spacing between content and the box (Padding) or spacing between objects (Margin).

15. When you are finished defining options for your Div, click OK. You can enter content in your positioned Div by clicking inside it and typing, or inserting images (**Figure 35d**).

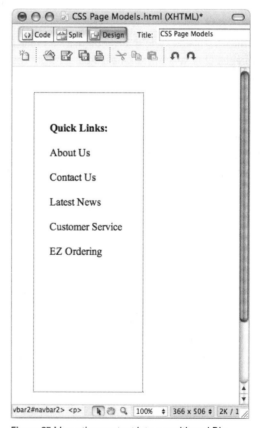

Figure 35d Inserting content into a positioned Div.

#36 Using Rulers, Guides, and Grids as Layout Tools

Since layers and definable Div tags allow you to design pages in an intuitive, interactive, graphical environment, wouldn't it be nice if you could use design features like rulers, guides, and gridlines to make it easy to align and place layout objects? Good news—you can!

Dreamweaver's rulers, guides, and gridlines display much like those in Illustrator, InDesign, and Photoshop. Combined with layers and definable Div tags, they complete the evolution of Dreamweaver's Document window into a graphical design workspace.

To display rulers in an open document, choose View > Rulers > Show. The View > Rulers submenu also allows you to choose between pixels, centimeters, and inches. (**Figure 36a**).

Figure 36a Choosing a unit of measurement for rulers.

You can even redefine the horizontal and/or vertical zero points for the rulers. Do this by dragging the icon at the intersection of the horizontal and vertical rulers onto the Document window page. The point at which you release your mouse becomes the new zero point for the horizontal and vertical rulers (**Figure 36b**). To reset the ruler zero points, choose View > Rulers > Reset Origin.

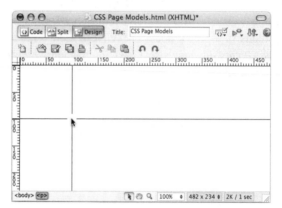

Figure 36b Setting a customized horizontal and vertical zero point for rulers.

To place a horizontal or vertical guide on the page, click and drag a ruler, and then drag it into the Design window (**Figure 36c**).

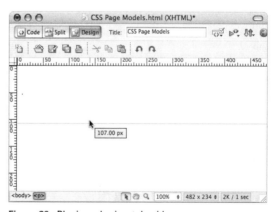

Figure 36c Placing a horizontal guide.

To edit the location of a guide, click and drag it. You can also double-click to edit the guide location or unit of measurement.

Guides can be locked to prevent accidental editing. (Choose View > Guides > Lock Guides). Guides can also be made "magnetic" so that they either snap to objects on the page, or objects on the page snap to them. To make a guide snap to elements on the page, choose View > Guides > Guides Snap to Elements. To make elements snap to guides, choose View > Guides > Snap to Guides. Clear guides by choosing View > Guides > Clear Guides.

Grids can be displayed by choosing View > Grid > Show Grid. Make grids "magnetic" by choosing View > Grid > Snap to Grid.

Define grid properties by choosing View > Grid > Grid settings. The Grid Settings dialog allows you to change the color of grid-lines, spacing between grids, grid display and snap properties, and display (dots or lines). Click Apply to preview changes to the grid, or click OK to close the dialog and change grid settings in the Document window (**Figure 36d**).

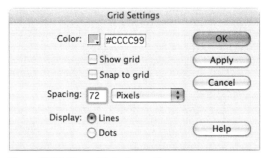

Figure 36d Editing grid display settings.

Rulers, Guides, and Grids for Design Purposes Only

Rulers, guides, and grids do not actually become part of your Web page. They appear in the Document window (in Design view only) to help you place or align objects.

Rulers, guides, and grids make it easy to place many layers or defined Div tags on your page, size them, and align them.

Regardless of what ruler, guide, or grid display you select in Dreamweaver, these elements *do not* display in a browser window.

Formatting Text

There are two kinds of text formatting in Web pages. The most basic and much less powerful method is assigning HTML tags to text, and then adjusting or enhancing the formatting by modifying those tags with *attributes*. HTML includes tags that define a document's structural elements, including headings (such as H1, H2, and so on down to H6) and the Paragraph tag. With HTML tags and attributes you can also control text's appearance, including font color, font size, boldface, italics, and underlining.

But there are limits to how much you can control the look of text using the tags available in HTML; what's more, current principles of good Web page construction recommend separating a content's structure from its appearance. In a nutshell, this means tagging page elements based on what they are (such as a paragraph or a block quote) rather than what you want them to look like (such as 12-point Times Roman italic, centered). A style sheet is where you store information about appearance, and using one makes it much easier to ensure a consistent look across your entire Web site, even if you have lots of pages and change your styles frequently.

CSS style sheets let you define line spacing, word spacing, or font size (beyond relative attributes like "large" or "small"), unlike HTML tags.

It's important to understand that when you format text in Dreamweaver, you are both assigning an HTML tag (like Paragraph, or Heading 1), *and* you are enhancing that tag with CSS styles.

As you apply formatting to text, Dreamweaver automatically creates what are called *class,* or *custom class* CSS styles. In Chapter 11, "Formatting Page Elements with CSS," you'll learn to create separate (external) files that store CSS style definitions that are applied to many pages. However, when you apply formatting to text in Dreamweaver's Document window, Dreamweaver automatically adds CSS style definitions to the page itself; the style information is not saved in a separate file.

#37 Applying HTML Tags to Text

HTML Tags— The Skeleton of Your Document

One good reason to use HTML tags that accurately reflect your document's structure is that some browsing environments either replace or don't use the CSS styles you assign to pages. For example, many sight-impaired people use customized style sheets that make text easier to read, or *reader* software that reads the content of Web pages aloud. In both cases, HTML tags are reinterpreted to assist users with receiving the page content.

Another good reason to carefully and consciously apply HTML tags to all text is that it helps make your pages look consistent if you use an external CSS style sheet to apply styles sitewide.

Finally, structural HTML tags, like H1 (Heading 1), H2 (Heading 2), and so on translate well if readers copy and paste content into word processors. In fact, this works in the other direction as well. For example, content created in Microsoft Word, which uses styles like Heading 1, Heading 2, and Heading 3, can be saved as an HTML page, and the styles will "translate" from print to Web.

CSS formatting is generally the most powerful and flexible way to format text. Before CSS was widely supported, text was formatted by putting style attributes inside HTML tags. Even styling text using HTML tags has been superseded by the more powerful CSS, basic structural HTML tags still serve as the foundation for Web text formatting.

To put it another way, you *could* enclose all the text in your document with the basic P tag, and then set up CSS classes to make your text elements look different. However, for many reasons, a sounder approach is to choose the appropriate tag for each of your type of text—for example, any of the six heading styles, the paragraph style, or bulleted or numbered lists. Then you can customize the look of these elements using with CSS. (The sidebar on this page explains more about why it's desirable to structure your HTML documents using the appropriate tags.)

To format text with an HTML tag to a paragraph in Dreamweaver, you don't have to select all the text in the paragraph. The tags available for this purpose are all block-level tags, which means they apply to *entire* paragraphs. This is true even if you used a line break (Shift + Enter) to create a new line within a paragraph.

With your cursor in a paragraph, choose a tag from the Format pop-up menu in the Property inspector (**Figure 37a**).

Figure 37a Assigning a Heading 1 tag to selected text.

Normal text uses the P (Paragraph) style. There are six heading styles (Heading 1 to Heading 6). Heading 1 is the largest, and Heading 6 is the smallest. Heading 1 is typically used for a page title. Heading 6 is often used for footnotes, legal notices, and other very small text. Other styles fit somewhere in between these extremes (**Figure 37b**).

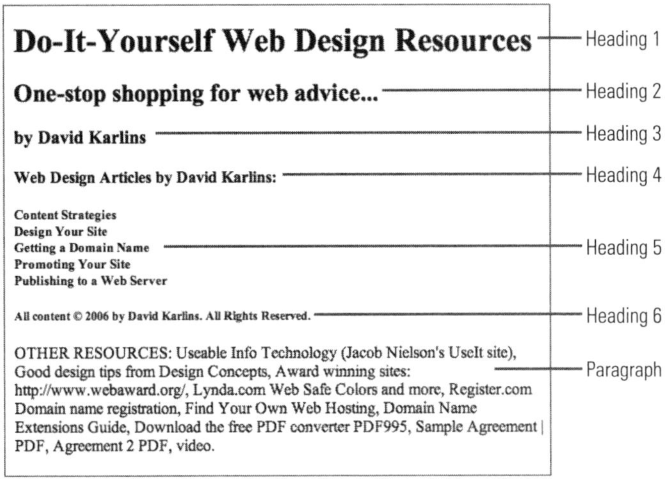

Figure 37b All six HTML heading styles applied to paragraphs.

In addition to the six heading tags and paragraph tag, you'll use a few other basic HTML elements to format text. They are all applied via buttons in the Property inspector and include:

- Bulleted list: Automatically applies bullet icons to paragraphs

- Numbered list: Automatically numbers paragraphs

- Boldface: Formats text with boldface

- Italics: Formats text with italics

- Indenting: Moves a paragraph away from the left margin

- Less Indenting: Moves a paragraph toward the left margin

- Align Left, Align Center, Align Right, and Justify: Define paragraph alignment

Boldface and italics are applied only to selected text. The other attributes are applied to entire paragraphs (**Figure 37c**).

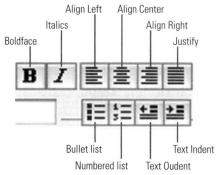

Figure 37c HTML formatting tags and attributes in the Property inspector.

#**38** Applying Colors to Fonts

Font color can be assigned to selected text. With text selected in the Document window, click the Text Color icon in the Property inspector to open the Text Color palette. You can choose from the array of "Web-safe" (widely supported) colors, or use the Eyedropper tool to pick up a color on your screen (**Figure 38a**).

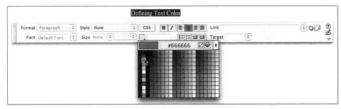

Figure 38a Assigning a color to selected text in the Property inspector.

Tip
Web-safe colors are especially relevant if you are primarily designing for handheld browsing devices, or other browsing environments that do not support thousands or millions of colors supported by modern computers.

To choose from color schemes (sets of selected colors) or to choose from the full range of colors supported by monitors, click the Color Wheel icon that appears at the top of the Text Color palette (this is the palette that appears when you click the Text Color icon in the Property inspector). When you click the Color Wheel icon, the Colors dialog opens. The Colors dialog has five tabs: Color Wheel, Color Slider, Color Palettes, Image Palettes, and Crayons. The tab on the left is the Color Wheel. Here, you can click any color in the spectrum of monitor-supported colors. The second tab from the left is the Color Slider tab, which is the most widely used tab in the dialog. Here you can easily define RGB colors interactively, or by entering R, G, and B values from zero to 255 (**Figure 38b**).

Colors on the Web

Colors are generated on monitors (or other viewing devices) by combining red, green, and blue dots on the screen. The RGB color system lists percentage of intensity for red, green, and blue dots.

The range of color available by combining red, green, and blue dots is wider than the range of color available for print. Therefore, images for the Web should use the RGB color mode.

Primitive monitors and computer graphics hardware did not support large numbers of colors. Therefore, all monitors support a small set of (216) "Web-safe" colors. However, as Web-safe colors became irrelevant with the development of new hardware and monitors, a plethora of other viewing devices (especially handheld ones) that do not support a wide range of colors has given new relevance to the old set of Web-safe colors.

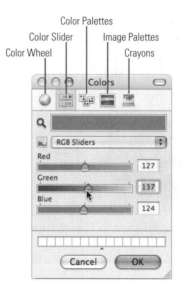

Figure 38b HTML formatting tags and attributes in the Color Slider tab of the Colors dialog.

There are other options in the Colors dialog as well. The Color Palettes tab allows you to access preset color schemes. The Image Palettes tab allows you to generate a set of colors from a Web image file (a GIF or JPEG file). The Crayons tab allows you to access a small set of colors represented as a box of crayons.

#39 Defining Inline Text Attributes with CSS

Building on a foundation of very few HTML formatting styles, CSS styles open the door to a range of typography that comes close to what is available in print—close, but not quite. The most important difference between Web and print typography is that when you apply fonts to Web pages, the fonts will only display correctly if they are installed on a visitor's browser. This means that when you use unusual fonts, most visitors will see a default font like Times Roman or Arial instead. However, with CSS you can define line spacing, word spacing, font size, font color, and other attributes.

To create a CSS formatting *rule* (style), click the CSS button in the Property inspector; the CSS panel appears. Here, you will create a CSS style that holds all the attributes you apply to the selected text. This style can be applied to other selections of text on the page as well. (I'll explain how to do this after I show you how to define a CSS style.)

Tip
You are defining a style with a set of formatting attributes. Later—after you define the style—you can apply that style to any text. It is not necessary to have text selected when you define the style.

If there is no CSS style already associated with the selected text, the CSS Styles panel appears with the Attach Style Sheet and New CSS Rule buttons active, and the Edit Style (and Delete CSS Property) icons grayed out. You can now create a CSS Rule (style), and later you can edit it (**Figure 39a**).

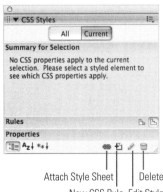

Figure 39a Defining a new style in the CSS Styles panel.

Attach Style Sheet | Delete CSS Property
New CSS Rule Edit Style

To create a new CSS style, click the New CSS Rule icon in the CSS Styles panel. The New CSS Rule dialog appears. In the Name field, enter a name for the style. In the Selector Type area, choose the Class (can apply to any tag) radio button; this defines a style that can be applied to any selected text. In the "Define in" area, choose the "This document only" radio button (**Figure 39b**).

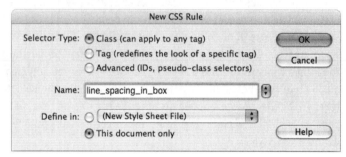

Figure 39b Creating a new style in the New CSS Rule dialog.

After you click OK in the New CSS Rule dialog, the CSS Rule Definition dialog opens (**Figure 39c**).

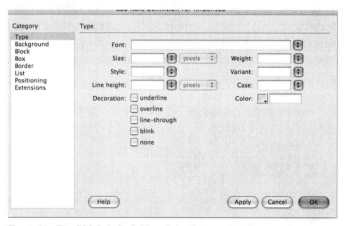

Figure 39c The CSS Rule Definition dialog for a new style.

The formatting options here are somewhat like those you are familiar with in your word processor:

- The Type category allows you to define font, size, weight (boldface or lightface), style (italic or Roman), and line height (line spacing). Line spacing can be defined as an absolute value or as a percent, so that 150% is one and a half lines of spacing between lines.

- The Background category allows you to define a background color or image behind the selected text.

- The Block category allows you to define features such as word spacing, letter spacing, vertical and horizontal alignment, and indentation.

- The Box category allows you to define positioning of CSS layout elements. See Chapter 7, "Page Layout with Layers and CSS," for an explanation of laying out pages with CSS.

- The Border category allows you to define the style (including solid or dashed lines), thickness, and color of borders around selected text.

- The List category allows you to define the style of bullets (circle or square), and numbering (roman or arabic).

- The Positioning category, like the Box category, allows you to define positioning of CSS layout elements.

- The Extensions category allows you to define page breaks, cursor display (when a cursor is moved over selected text), and special effects like blur and inversion. Page breaks apply to printed pages. Cursor display changes a visitor's cursor to a crosshair or other icon when he or she hovers over text. Blur and inversion effects are some of the less well-supported features of CSS formatting, and they require more knowledge of CSS than is possible to explore in this concise overview.

When You Need Absolutely Formatted Text

A theme that we return to from many angles in this book is that designing for the Web is less "fixed" and more relative than designing for print. You don't know the size of a visitor's "page" when he or she views your Web page—this depends on the visitor's computer and browser. You also don't know what fonts he or she has installed.

When you need to design a page that displays *exactly* the same way in *every* computer-based browser, the best options are either PDF or FlashPaper documents. Both PDF and FlashPaper retain original fonts regardless of viewing environment. The downside is that visitors require Acrobat Reader or Flash Player (both free downloads) to see the documents.

After you define a CSS style, you can apply it to selected text from the Property inspector. This is the easy part: Simply select text, and then choose a CSS style from the Style pop-up menu in the Property inspector (**Figure 39d**).

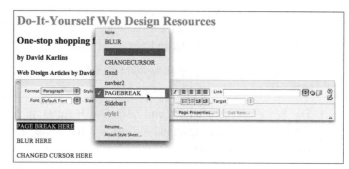

Figure 39d Applying a CSS style to selected text.

Embedding Images

Text and images are the basic building blocks of Web sites. Text is easy to add to a Web site; you can create text right in Dreamweaver or easily copy and paste any text from a document or Web page into a Dreamweaver document.

Pictures are more of a challenge. You can't create images in Dreamweaver or copy and paste images into a Dreamweaver document.

Now for the good news. There is a wide array of image editing programs—ranging from the one that came with your digital camera or computer operating system to Adobe Photoshop (or Photoshop Elements). Almost all of them can be used to prepare images for the Web.

Dreamweaver 8 includes some rudimentary image editing tools. But in general, you'll prepare images in advance (in another program) before you place them on a Web page. For that reason, #40, "Preparing Images for the Web," will explore a range of techniques available in programs other than Dreamweaver.

Once you have an image ready for your Web page, Dreamweaver makes it easy to place the image, align text to flow around the image, and assign links to either the entire image or part of the image (an image map).

#**40** Preparing Images for the Web

Web browsers recognize three types of image formats: JPEG, GIF, and PNG. The first step in preparing images for the Web is to save or export them to one of these formats. In general, the JPEG format is much better for photos; it supports a more complex set of colors than GIF or PNG. The advantage to using GIF and PNG formats is the ability to have a *transparent,* or invisible, background that allows the Web page background to show through. This creates the impression that the image is sitting directly on the page. The ability to make a color (usually the background color) invisible makes GIF or PNG the preferred format for icons and other graphics that show the page background "through" the image (**Figure 40a**).

Figure 40a A GIF image with a transparent color allows the page background to show through.

Can you get away with simply using a JPEG image file straight from your digital camera in a Web site? Maybe, but the file probably won't work well, even though the JPEG format available as an option in your digital camera is Web-compatible. The file is likely to be too large, both in dimensions and file size. And it is likely formatted for print, not Web display.

To prepare a file for the Web, you'll want to choose appropriate color, size, and resolution settings. Web images are generally saved at 72 dpi (dots per inch). This is much *lower* than print resolution (which is normally set to at least 300 dpi) because monitor resolution is 72 dpi on Macs and 96 dpi in Windows.

When you create images for a Web page, you generally try to keep file size small. File size is not much of an issue for print documents; nobody has to sit and stare at a printed book or newspaper waiting for an illustration to download. On the other hand, several 5 MB images on a Web page will take quite some time to download over a dial-up connection.

There are two ways to reduce file size: You can make the image smaller, or you can use *compression*. Smaller images are also smaller files, and they download quickly. Many Web sites use *thumbnail* images—small preview versions of a full-sized image. Visitors who want to see a full-sized version of the image, either on the same Web page or on a separate page, can click the thumbnail.

Thumbnail images address two challenges in Web design. They reduce the time it takes to download a page (compared to downloading full-sized images), and they help solve the problem of limited space on the page. It's generally a bad idea to place images on a page that won't fit in a standard-size browser window—roughly 800 pixels (8 inches) wide and 600 pixels (6 inches) high. Providing a set of clickable thumbnails that open full-sized images is a universally applicable technique for presenting images on Web pages (**Figure 40b**).

Thumbnails   Full-sized image opened by clicking a thumbnail

Figure 40b Visitors at Bruce Hopkins' Web site can click a thumbnail of an image to display the full-sized version.

#40: Preparing Images for the Web

Compression is a technique that reduces the number of pixels that need to be "kept track of" in an image file. This is done by defining only necessary pixels. So, for example, instead of "remembering" that there are 50 contiguous white dots in a photo, a compressed image file will define just one of these pixels and compress the file by simply noting that the other 49 pixels are identical to the defined one.

Compression can drastically reduce file size, speeding up download time. But compression also reduces quality by eliminating nuance in an image. The Save for Web window, available in Adobe products like Photoshop, Photoshop Elements, and Illustrator, allows you to preview images with different levels of compression, and compare them. The compression techniques in Adobe's Save for Web window are not crude; they are often very high levels of compression that drastically reduce file size without significantly affecting online quality (**Figure 40c**).

Figure 40c Comparing an uncompressed image with a highly compressed version of the same image. The photo on the left is one-tenth the file size of the original photo (on the right) and will download in 8 seconds, compared with almost 2 minutes for the uncompressed image on the right.

Tip

There are many good books on how to prepare images for the Web in Photoshop and Illustrator. If you like the approach and format of this book, check out Adobe Illustrator CS2 How-Tos: 100 Essential Techniques *by David Karlins and Bruce K. Hopkins, and* Adobe Creative Suite How-Tos *by George Penston.*

The final step in the process of preparing an image for the Web is to save the image file to the folder on your computer that you use for your Dreamweaver Web site. When you do this, it will be easy to find the image as you use it on your Web page.

#41 Embedding Images on a Page

Once an image is ready for the Web, you can embed it in a page in Dreamweaver. Why do I say *embed?* Because the image file remains a distinct file. To visitors to your Web site, it appears that the image is "part of the page." But in reality, a *separate* image file is displayed on your Web page using parameters you define in Dreamweaver that govern the location, size, and other elements of the image.

Start the process of embedding an image by clicking at the beginning of the paragraph of text with which the image will be associated, or in a table cell or CSS positioning element that you defined to hold the image.

Note

Defining page layout with tables is covered in Chapter 6, "Page Layout with Tables." Creating positioning elements with CSS is explained in Chapter 7, "Page Layout with CSS Layers."

With your cursor at the insertion point, choose Insert > Image. The Select Image Source dialog opens. Navigate to the image you want to place on the page, and click Choose (**Figure 41a**).

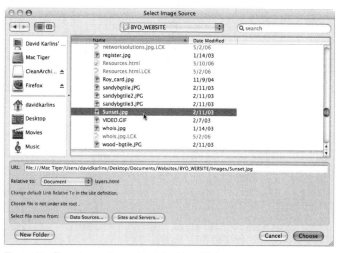

Figure 41a Choosing an image to embed in a Web page.

If the image file you selected is not in the folder you defined as your Dreamweaver site folder, Dreamweaver helpfully offers to save a copy of the image in your site folder. Click Yes in the dialog that appears to avail yourself of this service (**Figure 41b**).

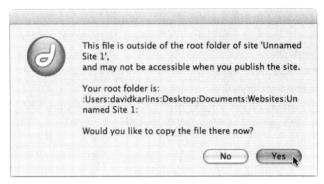

Figure 41b Saving a copy of an image file in your Dreamweaver site folder.

Don't Embed Images in the Middle of a Paragraph

Even if you want to display an image to the right of a line of text, embed the image at the *beginning* of the paragraph. Do this by placing the insertion cursor at the very beginning of the paragraph before choosing Insert > Image.

This might seem counter-intuitive, particularly if you're used to laying out images and text in a program like Adobe InDesign or Illustrator. But as you'll learn in #45, "Aligning Text and Images," the relation-ship of an image to a paragraph is a product of how the image is aligned, not of where it is inserted. Placing an image in the middle or at the end of a para-graph will make image and text alignment harder to control.

#42 Making Images Accessible with Alt Tags

Accessibility experts estimate that as many as 30 percent of all Web visitors rely on Alt tags. Visitors with various vision limitations use Alt tags to either replace or supplement what they can (or cannot) see. For instance, many color-blind visitors rely on Alt tags to supplement what they can see in an image. Additionally, many devices such as mobile phones and other handheld devices don't display images.

There are many reasons why visitors won't be able to, or won't want to see images in their browser. Visitors who rely on screen reader software to read your Web site content aloud will not see your image, nor will visitors using browsers on devices that do not display images. Other visitors to your site might have low-bandwidth connections and elect not to display images.

An Alt tag is code that is displayed if its associated image does not display in a browser window. In addition, with Internet Explorer and some other browsers, Alt tag text displays when you roll over an image with the cursor.

Well-designed Web pages provide Alt tags that display when, for any reason, an image does not display (**Figure 42a**).

Alt tag and image placeholder

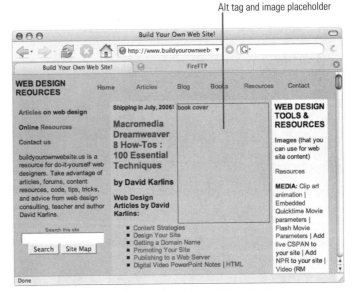

Figure 42a An Alt tag displays to identify a nondisplaying image.

Poorly designed Web pages that do not provide Alt tags simply display a tacky-looking *X*, question mark, or some other icon or symbolas an image placeholder when an image does not display. These sites are less accessible to visitors who are sight-impaired (**Figure 42b**).

Missing Alt tag

Figure 42b The image on this page doesn't have an Alt tag to identify its content.

You can define an Alt tag in the Property inspector by entering text for a selected image in the Alt field. Enter a brief description that will serve as an alternative for visitors who will not see the image (**Figure 42c**).

Alt tag field in the Property inspector

Figure 42c Alt tag text.

#42: Making Images Accessible with Alt Tags

Alt tags are more useful if they are not too long, thus the recommended maximum length is 50 characters. Sometimes that's not enough. For example, if you need to convey information depicted in a graph, map, or detailed photo, you might want to provide more information to visitors than fits in an Alt tag.

The solution is to provide a separate file that contains unlimited text. This file is accessed by the long description (longdesc) attribute. The content of a longdesc attribute is not text; it is the name of a Web page that contains a text description. The first step in providing a long description for an image is to create a separate all-text file that describes the image (**Figure 42d**).

Figure 42d Attaching a long description file to a selected image in the Tag panel.

Once you have created an HTML page with a long description for an image, access the longdesc attribute for a selected image by choosing the Tag inspector (choose Window > Tag Inspector). Expand the CSS/Accessibility category in the Tag panel, and use the Browse icon to navigate to the file you created with the long description.

#43 Editing Images in Dreamweaver

Dreamweaver's limited set of image editing tools allow you to crop, resample, change brightness and contrast, apply sharpening, and resize an image. When you select an image, Dreamweaver 's image editing tools will display in the Property inspector.

You can resize a selected image by clicking and dragging either the horizontal or vertical sizing handles on the image, or by clicking and dragging the corner handle. Holding down the Shift key as you resize using the corner handle maintains the original height-to-width ratio of the image. The new width and height are indicated in the W and H fields in the Property inspector. You can also enter width and height dimensions in the W and H fields. When you resize an image in Dreamweaver, the width and height display in boldface type in the Property inspector, and you can use the Reset Image to Original Size icon to revert to the original size (**Figure 43a**).

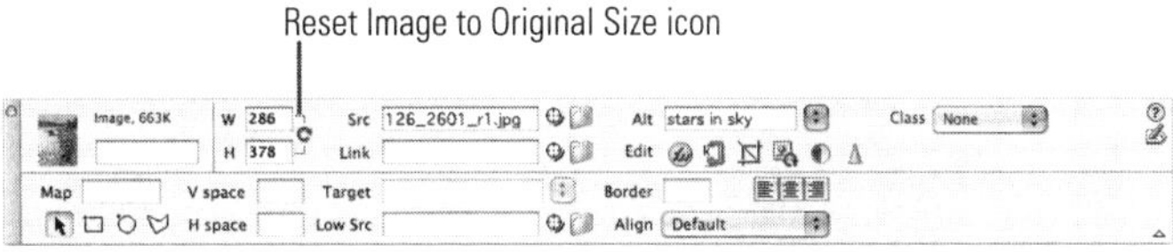

Reset Image to Original Size icon

Figure 43a Size indicated in the Property inspector.

The first two tools in the set, the Edit tool and the Optimize in Fireworks tool, launch a specified image editor, or launch Fireworks—an image editor that was part of the old Macromedia suite that was packaged with Dreamweaver before the Adobe acquisition.

The Crop tool, which works like a crop tool in programs like Photoshop, can be used to trim an image. The Resample tool reduces file size after you make an image smaller in Dreamweaver. Until you resample, the image displays in smaller dimensions on the Web page, but the file is not smaller. This means that the resized image will take the same amount of time to download that it did before it was resized. You can reduce file size and eliminate unnecessary pixels by clicking the Resample icon in the Property inspector. The Brightness and Contrast tool and the Sharpen tool will open dialogs with very simple sliders that adjust how an image looks (**Figure 43b**).

Drawbacks to Resizing in Dreamweaver

There are significant drawbacks to both enlarging and shrinking image dimensions in Dreamweaver. If you make an image larger, you will significantly degrade the quality of the image because there is not enough data saved in the image file to display more pixels. As a result, the image will appear grainy, blurry, or raggedy.

You will not lose quality in the same way if you make an image smaller. The image file will have enough data to display a smaller version of the image. However, the image quality will often still degrade because Dreamweaver's resizing tools are not sophisticated enough to figure out how to properly eliminate some of the image data.

Programs like Photoshop and Photoshop Elements have resampling features that intelligently add or remove pixels as you resize an image. In short, it's best if you can size your image before you bring it into Dreamweaver.

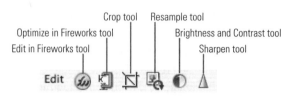

Figure 43b Image editing tools in the Property inspector.

To open the Brightness/Contrast dialog for a selected image, click the Brightness and Contrast icon in the Property inspector. Select the Preview Edit check box to see the effect of the changes you made to the brightness and/or contrast (**Figure 43c**).

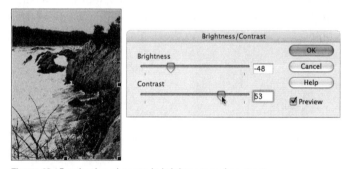

Figure 43c Previewing changes in brightness and contrast.

Similarly, the Sharpen dialog has a Preview check box so you can see the effect of the changes you made to the sharpness (**Figure 43d**).

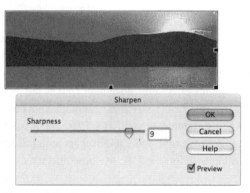

Figure 43d Previewing changes in sharpness.

#44 Generating and Using Thumbnails

Thumbnails are a valuable tool in presenting images on a Web page. They take very little space and download quickly, allowing visitors to preview a full-sized image by clicking the thumbnail.

As a legacy of Dreamweaver's Macromedia origins, Dreamweaver 8's utility for generating thumbnails automatically requires Fireworks (a trial version can be downloaded from Adobe).

With Fireworks installed, you can generate thumbnails for the images in a folder. The first step, then, is to copy all the images for which you want to generate thumbnails into a single folder.

The utility that generates thumbnails is actually designed to create a Web photo album (a slide show). The online photo album involves many files. Feel free to experiment with it, but in the process, this utility will create a thumbnail for every image in a specified folder.

To create thumbnail images from a folder of images, follow these steps.

1. In the Document window, choose Commands > Create Web Photo Album (it is not necessary to have a particular page open to do this). The Create Web Photo Album dialog will appear.

2. Unless you are generating a Web photo album, you can skip the first three fields in the dialog. In the Source images folder field, navigate to and select the folder that contains copies of all your full-sized images.

3. In the Destination folder field, navigate to and select the folder in which the generated thumbnails will be saved.

4. In the Thumbnail size field, choose a size (100 x 100 pixels is standard).

Note
The Show filenames check box is only relevant if you are creating a Web photo album.

(continued on next page)

Other Thumbnail Options

Photoshop also has a feature for converting a folder of images to thumbnails. Or, you can individually resize copies of images to use as thumbnails.

5. In the Photo format pop-up menu, choose a quality for the thumbnails.

There are two usable options here: JPEG—smaller file creates fast-loading, but poor-quality images, and JPEG—better quality creates thumbnails with more accurate color, but somewhat larger files and longer download time. If high-quality thumbnails are important to conveying your content, choose JPEG—better quality. If fast page opening is a priority, choose JPEG—smaller file. One consideration I take into account is *how many* thumbnails I will display on a page. If there are only a handful of thumbnails, I will usually choose high-quality JPEG. But if I am displaying 30 or so images on a page, high-quality JPEGs might take too long to download and drive visitors away.

Note

The two GIF options display too few colors for presenting photographs.

6. The other two options in this dialog (GIF webSnap 128 and GIF webSnap 256) are only relevant if you are creating a Web photo album. You can click OK, kick back, and relax while Dreamweaver (and Fireworks) create a set of thumbnails (**Figure 44a**).

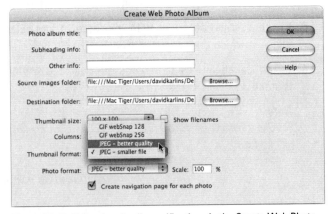

Figure 44a Defining thumbnail specifications in the Create Web Photo Album dialog.

#45 Aligning Text and Images

A flexible, reliable technique for combining images and text is to align an image either right or left. Aligning an image will flow text to the right (for a left-aligned image) or to the left (for a right-aligned image) of the image (**Figure 45a**).

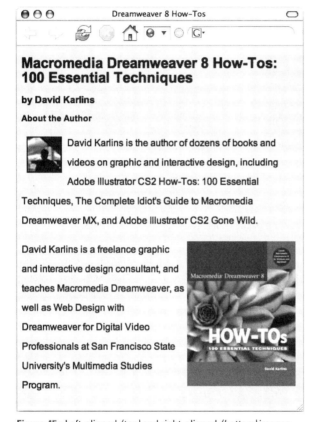

Figure 45a Left-aligned *(top)* and right-aligned *(bottom)* images.

You can also define a horizontal and vertical buffer space between images and the text that flows around them.

Aligned images are associated with a paragraph of text. They are not locked in place on the page, but instead move up or down on the page with the paragraph, depending on the size of the visitor's browser window.

Other Alignment Options

You might notice other alignment options in the Align pop-up menu besides Left and Right. These options are used to align tiny images that are supposed to appear in a line of text. The ability to do this is, in large part, a holdover from an era when operating systems did not support much in the way of symbols, and it was necessary to provide a way to embed and align tiny images within lines of text. Although these evolutionary relics are still available, they are not widely used and cannot be used to flow text around an image.

To align a selected image, click the Align field in the Property inspector and choose Left or Right from the pop-up menu (**Figure 45b**).

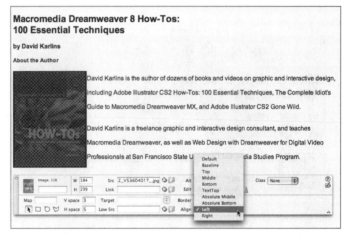

Figure 45b Left-aligning an image in the Property inspector.

When you align images in relation to paragraph text, you almost always want to define horizontal and vertical spacing to separate the edge of the image from the text. If you don't define horizontal and vertical spacing around the image, the image will bump into the text characters (**Figure 45c**).

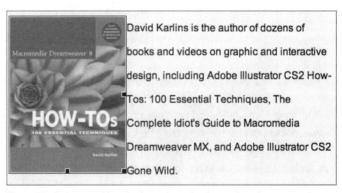

Figure 45c An image with no horizontal spacing bumps into the paragraph text.

You can assign vertical spacing to a selected image in the Property inspector by entering a value (in pixels) in the V space field. Assign horizontal spacing by entering a value (in pixels) in the H space field (**Figure 45d**).

Tip

A good standard setting for keeping images from bumping into text is 2 or 3 pixels of vertical spacing and 5 pixels of horizontal spacing.

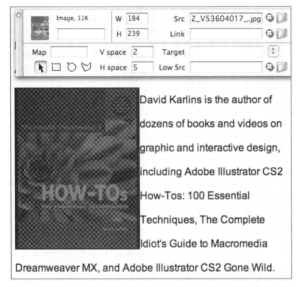

Figure 45d Assigning 2 pixels of vertical spacing and 5 pixels of horizontal spacing around an image.

Spacing around selected images appears as a blue line in the Document window. The blue line will disappear when you deselect the image.

#46 Defining Image Maps

In Chapter 5, "Creating Web Pages," I explain how to define links. Links can be launched from either text or images.

A single image, however, can contain more than one link. Breaking an image into sections, each with its own link definition, is called *creating an image map*. Image maps are used in a variety of Web graphics. One obvious example is an actual map, where a visitor can click a location (such as a state, city, or restaurant) and launch a link that opens a new page to display the area of the map where he or she clicked.

Image maps are often used to create navigation bars from a single image. A wide, thin graphic that stretches across the width of a page, for instance, can be divided into many links by creating multiple image maps on the same graphic.

Image map sections can be rectangles (including squares), ovals (including circles), or polygons (multisided shapes).

To create an image map from an image already embedded in your page, follow these steps:

1. Select the image to which the image map will be applied.

2. Click the Rectangular, Oval, or Polygonal Hotspot tool in the lower-left corner of the Property inspector (**Figure 46a**).

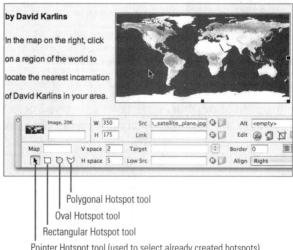

Polygonal Hotspot tool
Oval Hotspot tool
Rectangular Hotspot tool
Pointer Hotspot tool (used to select already created hotspots)

Figure 46a Hotspot tools in the Property inspector.

3. Draw a rectangle or oval by simply clicking and dragging the image with the appropriate Hotspot tool selected. Polygonal hotspots are a bit trickier. To define a polygonal hotspot, choose the Polygonal Hotspot tool, and click *(do not click and drag)* spots on the image. The hotspot is defined as you create additional points (**Figure 46b**).

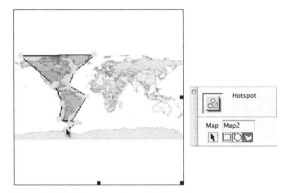

Figure 46b Defining a polygonal hotspot.

4. You can move a defined hotspot by selecting it with the Pointer Hotspot tool and dragging the whole hotspot. To delete a hotspot, select it with the Pointer Hotspot tool and press the Delete key. To resize a hotspot, select a single handle and drag it (**Figure 46c**).

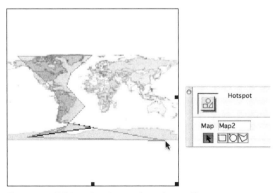

Figure 46c Editing the shape of a polygonal hotspot.

(continued on next page)

#46: Defining Image Maps

Zoom to Draw Hotspots

Drawing hotspots is a technique made much easier by Dreamweaver 8's ability to zoom in (or out). To zoom in, go to the Document window and choose View > Zoom In from the menu. To zoom to a set magnification, choose View > Magnification, and choose a magnification percent from the submenu.

By zooming in, you can draw accurate hotspots on an image. When you're finished drawing, choose View > Magnification > 100% to view the page as it will be seen in a browser window.

5. As soon as you finish drawing a hotspot, or if you select a hotspot with the Pointer Hotspot tool, the Property inspector adapts and displays properties just for the selected hotspot, not for the entire selected image (**Figure 46d**). In the Map field, you can name your map (or just accept the default name). In the Link field, click the blue Browse for File (folder) icon to navigate to a file in your Web site, or enter a URL in the field. In the Target field, choose _blank if you want the link to open in a new browser window. If you don't want to open the link in a new browser window, don't enter anything in the Target field. You can define a separate Alt tag for the hotspot by selecting a tag from the Alt menu. (For an explanation of Alt tags, see #42, "Making Images Accessible with Alt Tags.")

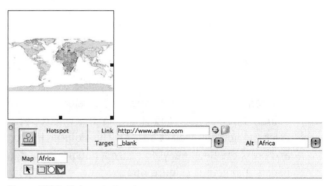

Figure 46d Defining a hotspot.

Hotspots are widely supported in browsers, but they appear differently in different browsers. Like everything involved in your Web pages, you should try to test your hotspots in several viewing environments.

Planning and Implementing Site Elements

If your Web site is just a handful of pages, you can manage the content on each page more or less independently. That is, you can open each page, one at a time, and edit content.

However, when your site is more complex than just a few pages (and most are), you'll find Dreamweaver's features for managing embedded site content essential.

Dreamweaver allows you to create page elements, such as navigation bars, page banners, icons, and bits of text (for example, a copyright notice), and then embed these elements in any of your site's pages. These elements can be text, images, or a combination of text and images. There are two different kinds of site elements in Dreamweaver:

- Template pages provide a common design for all pages to which they are attached.

- Library items are objects that are embedded in any number of pages.

Both template pages and library items are *updatable sitewide*. This means that if you embed a logo, copyright notice, text, or image (or a combination of text and images) in your pages and you edit the template or library item that defines that object, *all pages* that are created from the template or that have the library item embedded in them will update automatically.

This chapter explains how to create template pages, how to generate new pages from a template, how to define library items, and how to embed library items in pages.

#47 Creating Template Pages

The central concept in creating and using template pages is that they include *editable* and *noneditable* regions. Noneditable template page regions are parts of the page that are defined in the template; they can only be edited in the template file. Once they are edited, they apply to all pages with which the template is associated.

Let's explore a typical template page. The page might have a banner across the top, a navigation bar on the left, and a copyright/navigation bar at the bottom. The template defines these elements. A region in the middle of the page could function as an editable region—and would have different content on every page on the site (**Figure 47a**).

Noneditable regions

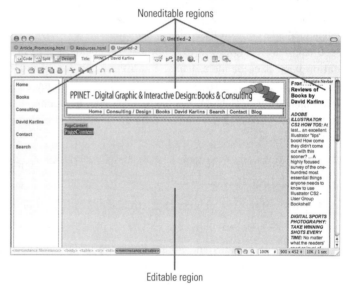

Editable region

Figure 47a A page that uses a template.

To create a template page, choose File > New to open the New Document dialog. Click General at the top of the dialog, and click the Basic page category from the list on the left. In the Basic page column in the middle of the dialog, click HTML template, and then click the Create button (**Figure 47b**). The template page will open.

Planning and Implementing Site Elements

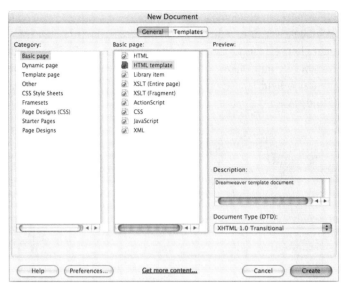

Figure 47b Creating a new template.

The Document window for a template page looks just like the Document window for a regular page, except that <<Template>> appears in the title bar of the window.

Just to review where we are in the process: At this stage, you are defining the template page. This page will then be used to generate an unlimited number of actual site pages, based on the template you are defining.

There are two steps to creating a template page. First, create all the *noneditable* elements that will appear on *every* page. Then, create the editable regions.

When you define template pages, you don't draw editable regions; you take existing page elements (such as a table, table cell, or CSS layer), and you make these elements editable when you use the template to generate new pages. Therefore, the standard strategy for creating a template page is to first create a page layout using either CSS layers or tables. You can then place noneditable content in tables or table cells (if you are designing with tables) or in a CSS layer.

To make an element on the page—like a table or table cell (or CSS layer)—into an editable region, click inside the element, and then choose Insert > Template Object > Editable Region. The New Editable Region dialog will open. Enter a name for the region in the Name field, and then click the OK button to define the region (**Figure 47c**).

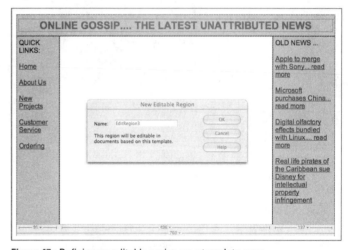

Figure 47c Defining an editable region on a template page.

In addition to editable regions, template pages can (but do not have to) include *noneditable* content. Any text, image, or media that you place on a template page that is *not in an editable region* becomes part of every page generated by that template.

You might, for example, have copyright information that appears at the bottom of every page generated by the template, or you might have contact information or a navigation bar on every page. You can include on a template page anything you can put on a regular Web page. Just keep in mind that any content that is not in an editable region will appear on *every* page generated using the template you are defining.

Once you have defined a template page with a noneditable region (if you wish to make it part of the template) and at least one editable region, you're ready to save the page and use it to generate an unlimited number of pages. Save the page by choosing File > Save. The Save As Template dialog will open. Enter a short description in the Description field, and enter a file name in the Save as field (**Figure 47d**).

Figure 47d Saving a template.

Note

By default, Dreamweaver will automatically create a Templates folder on your site and will save all template pages in that folder. Dreamweaver templates are saved with a .dwt file extension.

#48 Generating New Pages from Templates

To create a new page from a template, choose File > New to open the New from Template dialog. In the New from Template dialog, click Templates at the top of the dialog. In the "Templates for" column, click the site on which you are working (**Figure 48a**). You can preview any available template page by clicking it to see a thumbnail image of the template in the Preview area of the dialog.

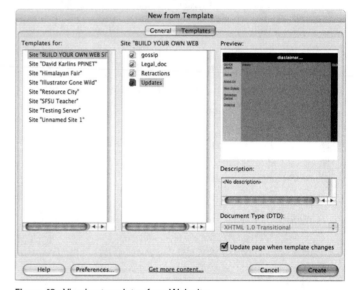

Figure 48a Viewing templates for a Web site.

Tip
The Update page when template changes check box is selected by default. Most of the point of designing with templates is that when you edit the template, all pages generated by that template will update to reflect the changes to the template file. So, normally you will leave this checkbox selected.

After you select a template, click the Create button in the dialog to generate a new page. The new page will include all noneditable content (images, text, or media) that is part of the template. To enter unique content for the generated page, click in the editable region for the template, and enter text, images, or other content.

Templates as a Web Design Tool for the Masses

In addition to saving time, page templates allow designers who don't know much about Dreamweaver to edit or create Web pages. In a typical setup, a design guru (like you!), will design the templates. Page formatting and many page elements are noneditable elements of the template. A single table cell, table, or CSS layer is set aside as an editable region, and novice designers can copy and paste text and/or place images in this editable region.

Adobe distributes a special program called Contribute that can be used *only to add or change content* in editable regions of Dreamweaver templates. Contribute is used in environments where many people are contributing content to a site that was designed by someone using Dreamweaver.

If there are multiple editable regions, click in every region and enter content (**Figure 48b**).

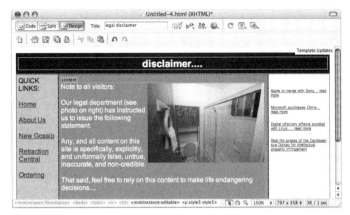

Figure 48b Entering an image and text in an editable region.

After editing the editable region on a template page, save the page by choosing File > Save. Assign a file name, and save the page as you would any Web page.

#49 Updating Templates

Updating Templates Takes Time

In this technique's scenario, I posed the hypothetical and exaggerated example of a Web site with millions of pages. However, even if your site has only hundreds of pages, Dreamweaver takes some time to update pages when a template is changed.

Then comes the slow part: After you update a template, you still need to upload all changed pages to your server. Because this is confusing to many people, I included a separate How-To at the end of this chapter on how to manage template updates at a remote server (see #53, "Uploading Templates and Library Items").

Your Web site consists of 2,304,451 pages. Okay, let's say it consists of 230 pages. In any case, consider this scenario: You need to change an element that appears on every page. That might be a newly designed company logo, an updated news notice, or a drastic personnel change.

In any case, you can easily update all the affected pages on your site in minutes by editing the template on which your site pages are based.

You can easily open and edit a template either from the file menu or from an open page that is associated with the template. If you have a page open that was generated from the template you want to edit, choose Modify > Templates > Open Attached Template.

If a page associated with your template is not open, choose File > Open, and navigate to the template file in the Open dialog (**Figure 49a**).

Figure 49a Opening a template page.

With the template page open, edit the *noneditable* regions (that is, any region that is not defined as an editable region). After you edit the page content, choose File > Save. The Update Template Files dialog will open. The dialog lists all files generated from the

Planning and Implementing Site Elements

template you are saving. If you only want to update some of the pages generated from the template, click (or Shift-click or Command/Ctrl-click) to select files to update. Then click the Update button to apply the changes in the template to all (or selected) pages (**Figure 49b**).

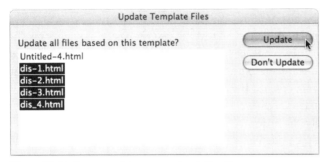

Figure 49b Saving a template page and updating files.

The Update Pages dialog will then appear. Here you can select the Show log check box to generate a list of affected pages (**Figure 49c**). After the update process is completed, click the Close button to close the Update Pages dialog.

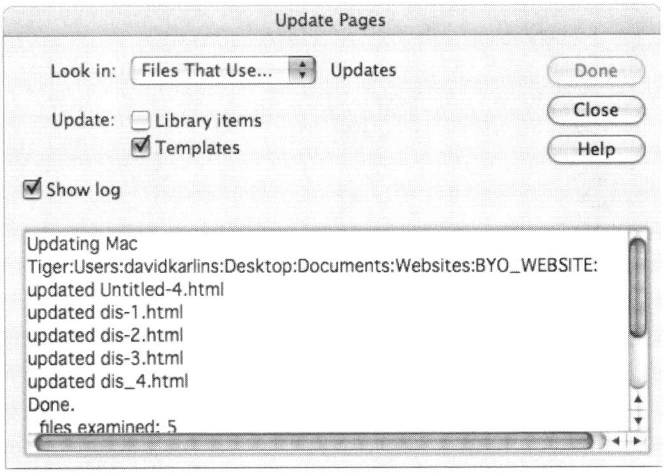

Figure 49c Viewing a log of updated pages.

#50 Creating and Embedding Library Items

Library items are like templates in that they are associated with pages and they update sitewide. They are different in that library items are *embedded in a page,* and they can be placed in pages generated by templates, in template pages themselves, or in just a regular Web page. Another way to think of it is that templates are entire pages, while library items are just individual elements that can be inserted into any page.

Library items can be text, images, or even media plug-ins (like a Flash animation), or they can be a combination of these. For example, if you want to place an article on every page or on several pages, you could embed the article as a library item. When the time comes to update or change the article, you can edit the library item and update the article on every Web page in which it is embedded.

You can define a library item two ways. You can drag content from an existing page into the Library window, or you can define library content from scratch in the Library window.

To drag existing content into the Library window, follow these steps:

1. Choose Window > Assets to view the Assets panel.

2. In the column on the left side of the Assets panel, click the Library icon (the last icon in the column). Any existing Library items will display (**Figure 50a**).

Figure 50a
Viewing the Library category of the Assets panel.

3. Click and drag to select the content on your page that will become a library item. Drag the content to the top window in the Library category of the Assets panel (**Figure 50b**).

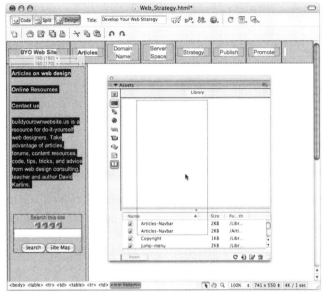

Figure 50b Dragging content to the Library category of the Assets panel.

Note

When you drag content to the Library tab, a warning dialog alerts you that the content may not appear the same when it is embedded in a page. See the sidebar on this page for an explanation of this occurrence.

continued on next page

Library Items Adopt the CSS Style of the Page in Which They Are Embedded

Library items may look different on different pages because they adopt the CSS styles of the page in which they are embedded. Normally, this is no big deal. If all the pages on your Web site use the same CSS styles for formatting, then the embedded library item will look the same on every page.

But there's another wrinkle in the process: If you edit a CSS style, it will change how the embedded library items with that style attached to them will appear on Web pages. This is not a bad thing; it just means that library items are governed by an external style sheet applied to a page the same way other page objects are.

See Chapter 11, "Formatting Page Elements with CSS," for an explanation of how to manage sitewide formatting with CSS.

4. Enter a name for the new library item by clicking the item in the Names list at the bottom of the Library category of the Assets panel and entering a new name.

You can also create a library item from scratch. There are four icons at the bottom of the Library category of the Assets panel:

- The Refresh Site List icon generates an updated list of library items associated with the open Web site.

- The New Library Item icon creates a new library item.

- The Edit icon opens a window to edit the selected library item.

- The Delete icon deletes the selected library item.

5. To generate a new library item, click the New Library Item icon (**Figure 50c**). A new item appears in the Library category of the Assets panel. Enter a name for the new library item (**Figure 50d**).

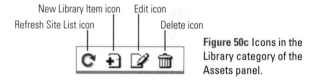

New Library Item icon   Edit icon
Refresh Site List icon   Delete icon

Figure 50c Icons in the Library category of the Assets panel.

Figure 50d Naming a new library item.

6. Once you create a library item, you can drag it from the Library tab of the Assets panel to any page on your Web site. Do this by simply dragging the library item to an open page in the Document window (**Figure 50e**).

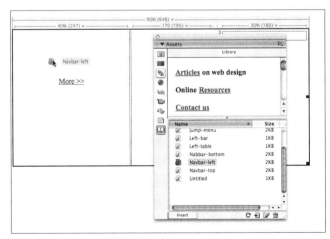

Figure 50e Dragging a library item to a page.

#**50**: Creating and Embedding Library Items

#51 Updating Library Items

When you edit a library item, the item will update on every page in which it is embedded. To edit a library item, click the item in the Library tab of the Assets panel, and click the Edit icon at the bottom of the panel. The library item will then open in the Library Item window, which looks like the Document window, except that the title bar includes <<Library Item>> (**Figure 51a**).

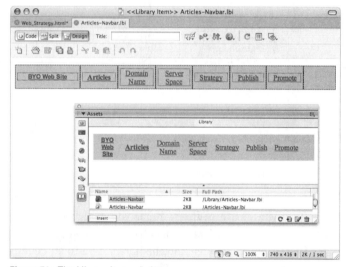

Figure 51a The Library Item window.

The Library Item window is just like the Document window, except that it is used to edit library items. You can edit in the Library Item window just as you can in the Document window. After you edit the library item in the Library Item window, choose File > Save to save your changes. The Update Library Items dialog will then appear with a list of all pages in which the library item is embedded.

You can select some of the pages in the list to update, or simply click the Update button to update the entire list (**Figure 51b**).

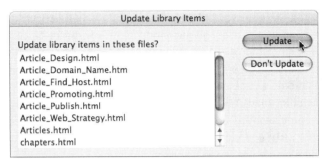

Figure 51b Updating pages with a library item embedded in them.

After Dreamweaver finishes updating pages with embedded library items, the Update Pages dialog will appear. You can select the Show log check box to see a list of all updated pages (**Figure 51c**).

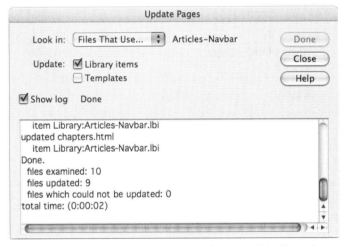

Figure 51c Viewing a list of updated pages with an embedded library item.

Library Items Can Include Anything

Library items are really HTML pages that are embedded in other HTML pages. Therefore, you can include text, images, and even media plug-ins in a library item.

Library items are saved with an .lbi file extension. They are proprietary objects in Dreamweaver—you can't edit a library item if you open a site with Go-Live or another Web editing tool.

#52 Including Navigation in Templates and Library Items

It's often useful to create templates with navigation bars in them, or with navigation bars that are library items that can be embedded in any page. Either way, you can automatically generate pages with working navigation bars using a template. Or, quickly pop a navigation bar onto a page by dragging a library item to that page.

Including navigation links in a template or library item *can* work, provided you are conscious of and correctly manage the folder structure of your site.

There are two ways to solve this problem:

- Keep *all* pages connected with the template *in the same folder* on your local site. They will then be transferred to the remote site with the folder structure intact, and the links will work.

- Use *absolute* links in the embedded library, or use template navigation links. Absolute links are defined by entering a full URL (like http://www.davidkarlins.com/aboutus.htm) instead of just a relative URL (like aboutus.htm).

The second option is less flexible. When you use template navigation links, it's harder to update links sitewide. Also, it reduces Dreamweaver's effectiveness in ensuring that links are not corrupted when you rename files.

To create a navigation bar that will work as part of a template page or as part of a library item, first organize into the same folder on your site all pages that will be targets of links in the navigation bar. You *can* create the navigation bar and link to files in multiple folders, but this complicates the process and requires you to keep track of more file folder locations than is necessary.

Tip
A navigation bar refers simply to a set of links (sometimes in a one-row, several-column table) or sometimes just a set of links separated by spacing or vertical bars ("|"). The essential point is that you can create this navigation bar and use it on many pages if you keep all pages that use the navigation bar in the same folder on your Web site. This way, you can use relative links from that folder to other files on your site, and the relative links will work on all pages using the shared navigation bar.

With all the target files in the same folder, you can generate new pages using the template page with the navigation bar, or you can place library items with navigation bars on pages (**Figure 52**).

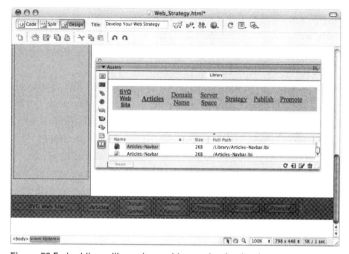

Figure 52 Embedding a library item with a navigation bar in a page.

Something else to keep in mind: Save in the same folder all pages generated by the template with a navigation bar, or all pages in which a navigation bar library item is embedded.

As long as the links are defined correctly for one page, you can use embedded library item navigation bars or template page navigation bars to easily create global uniform navigation bars on your pages. And these navigation objects can be easily updated, either by editing a template or by editing a library item.

Navigation Bars in Library Items and Templates: Pros and Cons

Because most Web pages have navigation bars of some type, and because those navigation bars are occasionally updated, it's very useful to include links in library items or page templates.

The downside is that if one of the links in your template or library item is bad, then *all* pages in which the library item is embedded (or all pages created using the template) will have corrupted links.

When this happens, however, you can fairly easily repair the problem. Just open the library item or template page, and redefine the link. Save the template or library item, update all the associated pages, and then upload the fixed pages to your server.

#53 Uploading Templates and Library Items

One of the things my clients and students (and fellow developers) find most disorienting in Dreamweaver is managing changes to templates and library items on a remote server.

Here's why: When you edit a library item (or template), all pages associated with that library item or template are automatically updated *on your local site*. These pages are not automatically updated *at the remote server*. Because this can be confusing and frustrating, I'll walk through the process.

When you save changes to an edited template, you are prompted to update all pages generated by the template. When you edit and save changes to a library item, the process through which the changes are made to every page is that you are prompted to save all changes to pages in which the library item is embedded.

This changes the pages on your local site. You *cannot* update the pages on your remote server by simply uploading the revised template or library page. In fact, it is not only impossible to update pages on a remote server by uploading a library item or template page, it also is unnecessary. You update the pages on your local server, and then you have to *upload all changed pages* to the remote server.

How do you keep track of which pages need to be uploaded to the remote server after you edit them by changing a template or library item? One way is to actually pay attention to the logs generated by Dreamweaver that list the changed pages. These logs can be copied and pasted into a word processor for easier management.

I usually use this trick: After I update files by editing a template or library item, I sort my files in the expanded Files panel by Modified date. Do this by clicking the Modified column title in the Files panel (**Figure 53a**).

Local Files		Size	Type	Modified ▼
	chapters.html	7KB	HTML File	6/9/06 12:...
	Articles.html	12KB	HTML File	6/9/06 12:...
	Article_Web_Strategy.html	17KB	HTML File	6/9/06 12:...
	Article_Publish.html	16KB	HTML File	6/9/06 12:...
	Article_Promoting.html	16KB	HTML File	6/9/06 12:...
	Article_Find_Host.html	13KB	HTML File	6/9/06 12:...
	Article_Domain_Name.htm	14KB	HTM File	6/9/06 12:...
	Article_Design.html	17KB	HTML File	6/9/06 12:...
▶	Library		Folder	6/9/06 12:...
	Web_Strategy.html	4KB	HTML File	6/8/06 11:...

Figure 53a Files sorted by the date on which they were modified.

With the files sorted by modified date, Shift-click to select all the files modified on the current date. Use the Put icon in the Files panel to put the files to the remote server (**Figure 53b**).

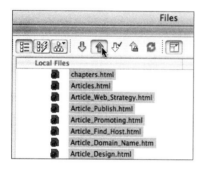

Figure 53b Uploading selected (recently changed) files.

Managing Local to Remote Transfers

Dreamweaver provides some sophisticated tools for uploading files to the remote server that match various criteria, including uploading all files that are newer on the local site than they are on the remote server.

These tools are explored in Chapter 16, "Testing and Proofing Tools."

Formatting Page Elements with CSS

In Chapter 7, "Page Layout with CSS Layers," and Chapter 8 "Formatting Text," I explained how to use CSS (Cascading Style Sheets) for page design and text formatting. Beyond controlling page positioning and text format, you can use CSS to format almost any element on a page.

You can use CSS to format:

- Body tags that define pagewide formatting, such as page background, margins, and default font color, type, and size.

- HTML tags ranging from images to tables.

- Links with special attributes.

- Special printable page formatting.

Formatting
#54 Page Elements with Style Sheets

Apply CSS to a Page or an Entire Site

All the CSS formatting techniques that you can apply to an external style sheet can be applied to an individual page (without an external file that stores formatting information). In other words, external style sheets don't have any special formatting tricks that aren't available by using CSS to define formatting on a single page. However, the magic of external style sheets is that you can apply them to as many pages as you wish—often all pages in a Web site.

Large, professional Web sites are formatted with *external style sheets*. External style sheets are files that define formatting for an unlimited number of Web pages. These files provide several levels of control over a Web site that cannot be achieved any other way:

- They ensure consistent formatting and a consistent look and feel throughout your Web site.

- They are a powerful productivity tool. They allow you to instantly attach a complex set of formatting rules to a new or existing Web page.

- They allow you to *update* or edit the look of an entire site almost instantly.

External style sheets are separate files, with a CSS file extension. You generate them automatically in Dreamweaver using the CSS Styles panel. You can open a CSS file in its own Document window and examine the CSS code if you choose. In any case, Dreamweaver takes care of creating and editing the CSS file as you define the CSS attributes.

The concept works like this: A single style sheet file (or sometimes a few files) stores all the information needed to format every Web page to which that style sheet is attached. When a visitor opens the HTML page to which a CSS file is attached, the browser automatically looks to the CSS file to find out how to display the page. This process does not take any noticeable time. Visitors to your Web site simply see a page with formatting, even though the formatting rules are stored in a separate (CSS) file.

The easiest way to generate a CSS (style sheet) file in Dreamweaver is to create a new style. As you do, you'll have the option of including that style in a new CSS file. In the following steps, you'll define a style and save it in a new style sheet. These steps can be adapted to generate a CSS file using any tag as the initiating style.

1. In the Document window, click the New CSS Rule icon at the bottom of the CSS Styles panel (**Figure 54a**). The New CSS Rule dialog will appear.

Figure 54a The New CSS Rule icon in the CSS Styles panel.

2. In the Selector Type area of the dialog, click a radio button to choose the type of style you wish to define.

   - Choose Tag to define formatting for HTML elements, such as headings, paragraphs, images, tables, or pages.

   - Choose Class to apply formatting rules, which are independent of tags, to any selected text.

   - Choose Advanced (IDs, pseudo-class selectors) to define links, among other things. If you are formatting a tag (e.g., H1—the Heading 1 tag), choose that tag from the Tag pop-up menu in the dialog.

continued on next page

3. Click the Define in radio button, and choose (New Style Sheet File) from the menu (**Figure 54b**).

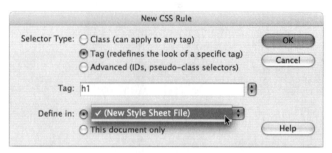

Figure 54b Generating a new style sheet.

4. Click OK in the New CSS Rule dialog. The Save Style Sheet File As dialog will appear. This is a typical Save As dialog, except that it automatically generates a CSS file with a *.css file extension and translates any formatting you define into CSS coding. Navigate to the folder in which you want to save the style sheet, and enter a file name in the Save As field. Then click Save to generate the new CSS file.

5. After you click Save, the CSS Rule Definition dialog for the style you are defining will open. Different categories in the Category list offer formatting options for different kinds of page elements. Now, simply note that there are a wide array of formatting options available, and that whatever formatting options you define will be encoded into the CSS file you named and saved in step 4 (**Figure 54c**).

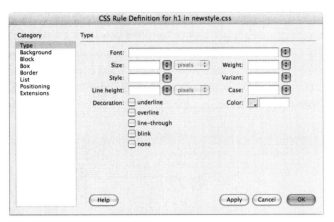

Figure 54c The CSS Rule Definition dialog.

Note

See Chapter 8, "Formatting Text," and especially #39, "Defining Inline Text Attributes with CSS" for an explanation of available text format options. Creating CSS rules for other page elements is explored in several techniques in this chapter.

6. After you create a style sheet file, the file is visible in the CSS Styles panel. When you expand the CSS file (click the triangle next to it to toggle to expand), all styles within the style will display. Formatting attributes display at the bottom of the CSS Styles panel (**Figure 54d**).

Figure 54d Viewing a CSS style in an attached style sheet in the CSS Styles panel.

Page Formatting Overrides External Styles

All CSS formatting can be either embedded in a single page or attached to that page via an external style sheet. In fact, the *Cascading* in Cascading Style Sheets refers in part to the fact that different levels of styles defer to each other. CSS applied to a page overrides CSS applied through an external style sheet.

This fact may set off an alarm for astute readers: If page formatting overrides formatting from external style sheets, the page formatting will "trump" the style rule applied via the attached style sheet. In other words, if you have *local* styles defined in a page, they override formatting applied by an attached external style sheet.

#54: Formatting Page Elements with Style Sheets

Styles Must Be Attached to Pages

After you create a style sheet for the first time, you can attach styles defined in that style sheet to any page. However, the page that you have open when you generate the style sheet file is automatically attached to the style sheet.

After you create a CSS file, you add styles to the file *without* creating a new style sheet. So, after you have created your first style and generated a CSS file, the *next* time you create a new style, click the New CSS Rule icon in the CSS Styles panel, but this time simply accept your already existing CSS file in the New CSS Rule dialog (**Figure 54e**).

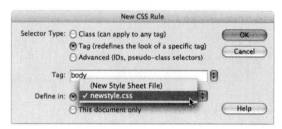

Figure 54e Defining additional styles for an existing CSS file.

As soon as you define a style in an external style sheet, that style is available to be attached to any new or existing page. To attach a style sheet to a page, open the page, and click the Attach Style Sheet (link) icon in the CSS Styles panel (**Figure 54f**). The Attach External Style Sheet dialog will open.

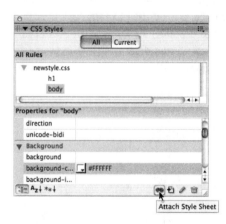

Figure 54f Attaching a style sheet to an open page.

Navigate to your CSS file, choose the Add as Link option, and click OK to attach the style sheet.

As you add and edit styles to the CSS file, all pages to which the CSS file is attached will update to reflect the new formatting.

#55 Formatting the Body Tag with CSS

The Body tag is a special tag. It underlies all other tags on a page. Think of the Body tag as the tag you will use to define page layout options such as margins and background color. The Body tag defines page background color (or pattern file), page margins, default font characteristics, and other attributes that apply to an entire page.

The Body tag is a powerful sitewide formatting tool. You can actually define most of the formatting for your site using the Body tag.

For example, if you defined the Body tag to display default text in dark gray Arial font, then *all* styles included in the style sheet would by default appear in dark gray Arial font. Heading 1 (H1) text would be larger than Paragraph (P) text. All text would be dark gray Arial font by default.

Also, since the Body tag defines page background color, this is another way in which this one style can control much of your site's appearance.

To define a style for the Body tag that establishes a default font, a page background color, and margin specs, follow these steps:

1. Click the New CSS Rule icon in the CSS Styles panel. The New CSS Rule dialog will open.

2. In the Selector Type area of the dialog, click the Tag radio button. From the Tag pop-up menu, choose body (**Figure 55a**).

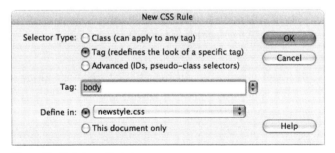

Figure 55a Defining a Body tag.

continued on next page

Don't Define Too Much

Normally, when you define a Body tag, you won't define font size or attributes such as italics or boldface. Remember, a Body tag provides the *basic* default formatting for text. You'll want different tag styles to look different, and normally you'll define font size as you define the Paragraph tag (P) and heading tags (H1, H2, and so on). Any attributes you define for these tags will override the Body tag definition.

3. In the Define in area of the dialog, choose either an existing or new CSS file from the pop-up menu (both options are available), or click the This document only radio button to define a Body tag that will format only the currently open page.

4. Click OK in the New CSS Rule dialog to open the CSS Rule Definition dialog for your Body tag. In the Type category, choose a font from the Font pop-up menu.

5. In the Background category of the CSS Rule Definition dialog, choose a swatch from the Background color area to select a background color for your page(s) if you want something other than the default white color (**Figure 55b**).

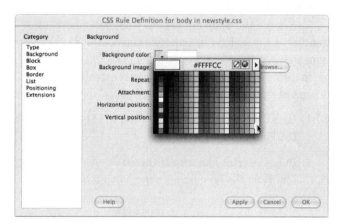

Figure 55b Defining page background color.

6. If you wish, you can define a tiling background image instead of a background color. Do this by clicking the Browse button to locate and choose an image file.

7. Different browsers display different default page margins. To define a set margin, select the Box category in the CSS Rule Definition dialog, and enter values for top, left, bottom, and right margins (**Figure 55c**).

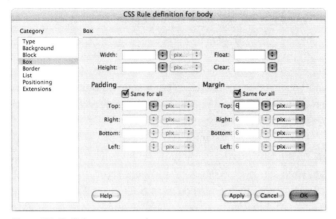

Figure 55c Defining page margins.

Using Page Background Images

If you choose to define a background image as part of the Body tag style, the image will *tile*, that is, it will repeat itself horizontally and vertically to fill the page. Graphic designers create special background images that tile smoothly to create a seamless looking background.

Why not use a background image large enough to fill the entire page? Such an image would not tile, but it would radically increase page download time. For this reason, background images are generally small (100 square pixels or smaller) and tiled.

#56 Formatting HTML Text Tags with CSS

There are six HTML heading styles: H1 (Heading 1) to H6 (Heading 6). Defining custom styles for these heading styles and the Paragraph tag is at the heart of designing a look and feel for your Web site. If you have formatted print documents with programs like Adobe InDesign, QuarkXPress, or even Microsoft Word, you probably understand the basic concept of defined styles. This concept applies to Web design as well.

Defined styles provide uniform text formatting, either on a page or, when the styles are defined in an external style sheet, throughout your site. For example, every major heading on your site might be 14-point Arial and purple. All paragraph text might be 10-point Arial, dark gray, and double-spaced.

Before walking through the process of defining CSS styles for HTML tags, it might be helpful to quickly review the difference between styles for HTML tags and *class* styles that are independent of HTML tags. In the introduction to Chapter 8, "Formatting Text," I explained how to generate what is called a *custom* or *class* style to apply a set of formatting rules to any selected text. Actually, by default and behind the scenes, Dreamweaver 8 automatically generates custom class styles whenever you apply formatting like font, size, or color to selected text using the Property inspector. These custom class styles can be applied to any selected text. The drawback, in contrast to HTML tag styles, is that custom class styles do not apply automatically to any text, while HTML tag styles automatically attach themselves to any text with that tag. All text you enter will normally have the Paragraph tag, so when you define a style for the Paragraph tag, the tag is automatically applied to much of the text on your page or Web site.

To prepare your site for CSS formatting applied to paragraph and heading text, the first step is to go through your Web page(s) and assign HTML tags to text if you have not done so already. This is covered in #37, "Applying HTML Tags to Text."

With HTML tags applied to text on your page(s), you're ready to define CSS styles that will apply to these tags. To do this, follow these steps:

1. Click the New CSS Rule icon in the CSS Styles panel (**Figure 56a**). The New CSS Rule dialog will open.

Figure 56a Creating a new style by clicking the New CSS Rule icon in the CSS Styles panel.

2. Here, you will first choose an HTML tag for which you will define a style. In the Selector Type area of the dialog, Click the Tag radio button. From the Tag pop-up menu, choose the tag for which you are defining a style (**Figure 56b**).

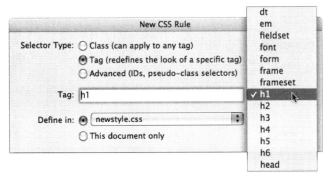

Figure 56b Defining a new Heading 1 (H1) style in the New CSS Rule dialog.

continued on next page

#56: Formatting HTML Text Tags with CSS

CSS Formatting Options

The following are some of the more useful formatting options available in the CSS Rule Definition dialog:

- The Type category defines font, size, weight, style (italic or Roman), and line height.

- The Background category defines a background color or image behind type.

- The Block category defines features such as word spacing, letter spacing, vertical and horizontal alignment, and indentation.

- The Box category defines positioning of CSS layout elements.)

- The Border category defines the style, thickness, and color of borders around text.

- The List category defines the type of bullet, or numbering.

- The Positioning category, like the Box category, defines positioning of CSS layout elements.

- The Extensions category defines page breaks, cursor display (when a cursor is moved over selected text), and special effects like blur or inversion.

How Many Heading Styles Do You Need?

Define CSS styles for as many HTML tags as necessary. Some designers find that defining two or three heading styles (like H1 and H2) is sufficient. I rely on all six heading styles, often reserving headings like H6 for special elements like copyright or legal notices.

3. In the Define in area of the dialog, choose either a style sheet from the menu, or choose the This document only radio button.

Note

See #54, "Formatting Page Elements with Style Sheets" for an explanation of defining styles in external style sheets.

4. Click OK in the New CSS Rule dialog to open the CSS Rule Definition dialog. The formatting options here may be familiar if you have been working with formatting in Dreamweaver. If not, a summary of available formatting options is in a sidebar in this technique.

5. After you define a CSS style, you can click the Apply button in the CSS Rule Definition dialog and see how the style looks when applied to the page. When you finish defining a CSS style for a tag, click OK. The style definition is automatically applied to an external style sheet, or to your page (depending on the selection you made in the Define In section of the New CSS Rule dialog when you began defining the style).

#57 Formatting Page Elements with CSS

In addition to defining CSS styles for HTML text tags (like paragraph or heading text), you can also use CSS styles to define the appearance of *any* HTML tag. This can get somewhat complex and can involve CSS formatting that is beyond the scope of this book. But you can also define CSS styles for commonly applied tags, like images or tables.

It often makes sense to define styles for the Image (IMG) tag and the Table (Table) tag. You can define border thickness, color, background color, and other features of tables or images.

To define a style for the Image or Table tag, follow these steps:

1. Click the New CSS Rule icon in the CSS Styles panel. The New CSS Rule dialog will open.

2. In the Selector Type area of the dialog, click the Tag radio button. From the Tag pop-up menu, choose the tag for which you are defining a style. The Image tag is img. The Table tag, intuitively enough, is table (not shown) (**Figure 57**).

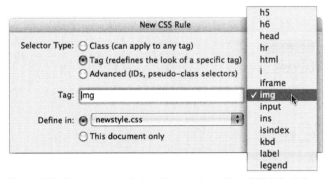

Figure 57 Defining a new style for all images in the New CSS Rule dialog.

3. In the Define in area of the dialog, choose either a style sheet from the menu, or click the This document only radio button.

Note
See #54, "Formatting Page Elements with Style Sheets" for an explanation of defining styles in external style sheets.

continued on next page

Do You Want to Apply CSS to Table and Image Tags?

Maybe. Keep in mind that if you apply a style to the Table tag—for example, a yellow background color—that style applies to *all* tables on your site (assuming you are using an external style sheet). I find this a bit heavy-handed. I like to apply different background colors to tables within my site, so I usually don't define a table style. When I manage very large sites, I usually define a CSS style for the Table tag because I don't want or need to custom-define background colors for every table.

On the other hand, I normally define a style for images. I'll use a style to define the border thickness and color that appears around the images. I like to keep this style standard throughout my site.

4. Click OK in the New CSS Rule dialog to open the CSS Rule Definition dialog. Many formatting options (like those applying to text) are not usually relevant for defining image or table properties. But you will likely want to use formatting options from the Background, Border, and Extensions categories. (See the "CSS Formatting Options" sidebar in #56 for more information on these styles.)

5. After you define a CSS style, you can click the Apply button in the CSS Rule Definition dialog and see how the style looks when applied to the page. When you finish defining a CSS style for a tag, click OK. The style definition is automatically applied to an external style sheet, or to your page (depending on the selection you made in the Define In section of the New CSS Rule dialog when you began defining the style).

#58 Applying CSS to Links

CSS formatting is applied to links so ubiquitously that sophisticated Web browsers expect to find features like rollover display or nonunderlined links on sites.

Let's go back in time for a moment to put this in perspective. By default, links display as blue underlined text. Visited links display as purple underlined text. Active links (links currently being followed) display as red underlined text. These defaults are defined by HTML and recognized by browsers.

For more flexibility in defining links, it is necessary to define CSS styles for links. CSS formatting allows you to define four link states. In addition to the three HTML states (regular, visited, and active links), CSS can define a fourth state—hover. Hover state displays when a visitor hovers his or her mouse cursor over the link.

There are many style approaches used for hover link formatting. Sometimes designers turn off underlining for all other link states but will have it appear when a visitor hovers over a link. Other times, designers define a color or background-display change when a link is hovered over (**Figure 58a**).

Figure 58a The background appears when a visitor hovers over the link.

Normally, you will *not* define font or font size to link style definitions. That's because links adopt the font and font size of the HTML formatting tag assigned to the text. For example, Heading 1 (H1) text might include text that is a link. Or, paragraph text might include some text that functions as a link. In either case, the font and font size will not change for the link text.

What normally *will* change is font color, and maybe font attributes like underlining or background. So, when you define CSS styles for links, you will normally avoid defining font or font size and instead define font color and special attributes (like underlining or background).

Should Links Be Underlined?

There are two schools of thought on whether or not links should always appear with underlining.

The "accessibility" school argues that underlined links in default colors (blue for unvisited links, purple for visited, and red for active) is universally understood, and makes links as unambiguous and accessible as possible for a wide range of visitors in the largest set of viewing environments.

The "aesthetic" school argues that such default-colored, underlined links are boring, traditional, and unnecessary—that today's sophisticated Web visitors can distinguish links as long as consistent formatting (usually a unique font color that is used only on links) is applied.

Between the two extremes, you have the option of having links that, for example, display underlining when rolled over or that use the traditional blue color, but do not display underlining.

To create a CSS formatting *rule* (style) for links on a page (or in a Web site, via an external CSS file), follow these steps:

1. With a page open, click the New CSS Rule icon in the CSS Styles panel. The New CSS Rule dialog will open.

2. In the Selector Type area of the dialog, click the Advanced (IDs, Pseudo-Class Selectors) radio button. From the Selector pop-up menu, choose one of the four link states: Link, Visited, Hover, or Active.

Note
You will define each of the four link states separately. Link (unvisited link), Visited, Hover, and Active are each a unique style.

3. In the Define in area of the dialog, choose either a style sheet from the menu, or click the This document only radio button to define styles that will be applied only to the open page (**Figure 58b**).

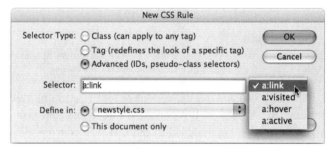

Figure 58b Defining an unvisited link style.

4. Click OK in the New CSS Rule dialog to open the CSS Rule Definition dialog for the link state you are defining. The formatting options you are likely to use for a link state are as follows:

- The Type category allows you to define a color for the selected link state using the Color box. The check boxes in the Decoration area allow you to turn underlining on or off. By default, links are underlined, so select the None check box to turn underlining *off*. Simply deselecting the Underline check box will not turn underlining off (**Figure 58c**).

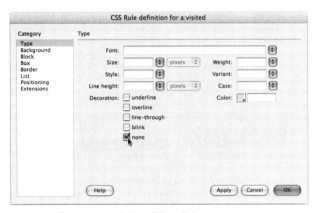

Figure 58c Turning underlining off for a link state.

- The Background category allows you to define a background color or image behind the selected text.

5. After you define a CSS link style, click OK to automatically apply it to an external style sheet or to your page (depending on the selection you made in the Define In section of the New CSS Rule dialog when you began defining the style). However, you will not see the effect of any link state other than link (unvisited) until you preview your page in a browser. To do this, choose File > Preview in Browser, and if more than one browser is available, choose a browser from the submenu.

#59 Defining CSS for Printable Pages

Many times, you will want to define different styles for printed pages than you use for monitor display. For example, you might change a light-colored font to black for printing or remove page or table background images.

You do this by creating and attaching a separate CSS file—a separate external style sheet—that holds print formatting rules. You can also preview how a page will look when printed in the Document window.

To define a new style sheet for printer output, you can create an external style sheet with CSS tag styles, link styles, or even class styles. Then you name the external style sheet that contains the print styles print.css (**Figure 59a**).

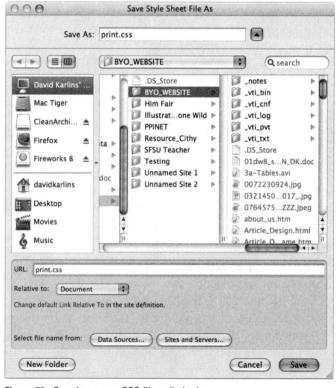

Figure 59a Creating a new CSS file called print.css.

Formatting Page Elements with CSS

Tip

Review the other techniques in this chapter for all the information you need to create an external style sheet.

After you define a distinct set of printable styles in the print.css style sheet file, attach the print.css file as the printer style sheet following these steps:

1. Open the Web page to which the printer CSS styles will be attached.

2. In the CSS Styles panel, click the Attach Style Sheet icon.

3. In the File/URL field of the Attach External Style Sheet dialog, click Browse and navigate to the print.css file. In the Add as area, leave the Link radio button selected.

4. From the Media pop-up menu, choose print (**Figure 59b**).

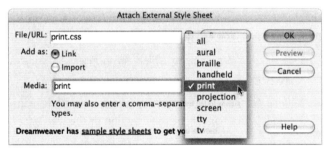

Figure 59b Defining print.css as the print media style sheet.

You can attach multiple style sheets to a page and define different CSS files to different media using the same process. To preview your printer styles, click the Render Print Media Type icon in the Style Rendering toolbar (**Figure 59c**).

Useful Print Formatting

Useful special formatting features for printed versions of pages include:

- No colored print—Many people print documents on laser printers that print only in black.

- No backgrounds—They interfere with readability.

- Different margins—They accommodate standard 8½-inch-wide paper.

- Page breaks—They break content into discrete sections.

If It's Not Broken...

You can choose any spot on your page as the place where you will force a page break on the printed page. Of course, you do not have to define a set page break; by default, a visitor's printer will, of course, print a long Web page on multiple pages. But defining a page break manually allows you to force a page break before the printer would normally produce a page break.

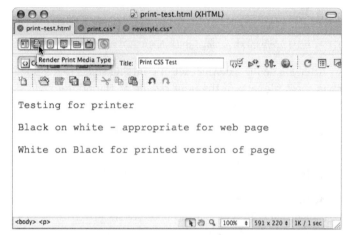

Figure 59c Previewing the applied print style sheet.

One Class Style attribute that is only relevant to print style sheets is the page break attribute. To define a page break in the printed version of a Web page, follow these steps:

1. Open the Web page to which the printer CSS styles will be attached.

2. Click to place your insertion point where the page break should occur on the printed version of the Web page.

3. Click the New CSS Rule icon in the CSS Styles panel. The New CSS Rule dialog will open.

4. In the Selector Type area of the dialog, click the Class (can apply to any tag) radio button. From the Name pop-up menu, choose a style name, such as page_break.

5. In the Define in area of the dialog, choose your print.css external style sheet from the pop-up menu.

6. Click OK in the New CSS Rule dialog to open the CSS Rule Definition dialog (**Figure 59d**).

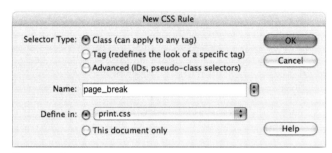

Figure 59d Creating a page break style.

7. In the Rule Definition dialog, choose the Extensions category. In the After field, choose Always from the pop-up menu (**Figure 59e**).

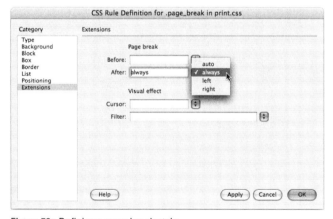

Figure 59e Defining a page break style.

After you define a page break style, you can apply it anywhere by inserting the style from the Property inspector (**Figure 59f**).

Figure 59f Inserting a page break style.

#60 Updating Sites with CSS

Let's start with the bad news. If you have created a huge Web site with hundreds or even thousands of pages and have *not* attached a style sheet or multiple style sheets to the pages, Dreamweaver does not offer a quick one-step process for this. So, attach style sheets *as you create pages*.

Now, the good news. Once you have attached a style sheet to multiple pages on your Web site (even thousands of pages), you can instantly update the appearance of the pages by editing your style sheet.

Here's how:

1. Open any page that has the style sheet attached.

2. In the CSS Styles panel, click the triangle next to the attached CSS file to toggle to expand it. A list of files will display (**Figure 60**).

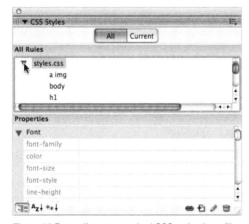

Figure 60 Expanding an attached CSS style sheet file and viewing styles associated with the style sheet.

continued on next page

How Do Styles Update So Fast?

When a Web page opens in a browser (and when you view a page in the Dreamweaver Document window), the formatting on that page reflects the attached CSS style sheet file. If you were to examine the HTML coding on a Web page (and you don't need to), you'd see that the line of code identifying the attached style sheet is near the top of the page of code. Browsers read this code and apply the appropriate style sheet file as they open the page.

When you update a CSS file, you don't actually edit the content or even the formatting of a page per se, but the changes you make to the file are immediately visible on any page to which the file is attached.

3. There are several ways to edit style attributes. In the bottom half of the CSS Styles panel, the Properties area displays formatting for selected styles. You might find it intuitive to simply double-click any of the formatting attributes to edit the style. Or, you can double-click the style itself in the All Rule area in the top half of the panel to open the CSS Rule Definition dialog, and edit the style in that dialog. (This familiar dialog looks just like the one you used to define the style).

4. When you click OK in the CSS Rule Definition dialog (or make changes in the bottom half of the CSS Styles panel), the changes are automatically applied to all pages to which the edited style sheet file is attached.

#61 Managing CSS Between Local and Remote Sites

In #60, I emphasized how quick and easy it is to update an entire Web site by editing a CSS file. While this is true, it's also the case that high up on the list of student frustration issues is the fact that updating a CSS file on a *local* site does not necessarily update the CSS file on a *remote* site.

When you update a Web page on a local site and choose File > Save to Remote Server, the Dependent Files dialog will open and you will be prompted to upload "dependent" files. If you select Yes in the dialog, the CSS files that are linked (attached) to your Web page will be uploaded along with the Web page itself. This is helpful because it ensures that updated styles are sent to your Web site along with the revised Web page (**Figure 61a**).

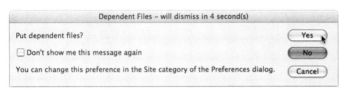

Figure 61a Uploading dependent files with a Web page.

You can also upload a CSS file directly to the server. Do this by selecting the CSS file(s) in the Files panel (use the F8 function key to toggle the display of the Files panel on or off). With the CSS files selected, click the Put File(s) icon to upload the files (**Figure 61b**).

Figure 61b Uploading CSS files in the Files panel.

To summarize, there are two approaches to uploading style sheets to your site. You can upload them as dependent files as you upload Web pages, or you can upload them separately. Understanding both of these options will help you troubleshoot when your styles are not reflected correctly in the appearance of pages on your remote server.

The Ultimate Backup

As the "ultimate backup," you should design Web pages so that if the style sheet link is broken for whatever reason, the site still functions. Don't rely on styles to convey essential information. For example, do not create white text on a black background; if a visitor's browser does not support the black background, he or she will only "see" (or more to the point, *not* see) white text on a white page. On the other hand, if you place red text on a yellow background, a visitor will see that red text on a white page even if the yellow background is not supported by his or her browser. If for some reason your style sheet link is broken or corrupted at your remote server, visitors will see the default style.

Designing with Frames

Frames allow you to display more than one Web page in a browser window. You can accomplish this by generating a special kind of Web page that has no content of its own, but simply serves as a container to display other Web pages that are embedded in *frames* within that container page. The whole *set* of HTML pages that work together to present more than one page in a browser are referred to as a *frameset*.

There are distinct advantages to designing with frames. Since each frame within a frameset is a separate Web page, visitors can scroll (usually vertically) within one frame, while continuing to view content undisturbed in a separate frame. Many artists and designers, for instance, use frames to display their portfolios—they use a frame on the left side of the page to allow visitors to scroll vertically down a long set of thumbnail images, and then much larger images display in a wider frame on the right side of the page.

Frames can also help reduce download time for Web pages, because page content in one frame does not have to reload when new content is displayed in another frame.

There are also significant disadvantages to designing with frames. One is that frames tend to confuse search engines, which identify content in HTML pages, not in combined frames. Visitors might end up following a search link to an HTML Web page that is intended to be displayed within a frame, and therefore see only part of the page content. Frames also pose accessibility problems for visitors with handheld browsing devices, and Web surfers who rely on reader software to read page content aloud.

Because frames open up design possibilities that cannot be easily accomplished with other page design techniques, they remain a viable element of page design.

#62 Generating a Frameset from Dreamweaver Designs

If you are like most of my students and clients, keeping track of files is not your favorite part of designing a Web site. Dreamweaver manages most file issues quietly and carefully, but the problem of handling files is multiplied when you work with frames. That's because frames consist of at least three HTML pages—a page that serves as a container for the whole frameset, and at least two embedded frame pages. Often one of the embedded pages is used as a navigation page, and the other is often referred to as the main frame (**Figure 62a**).

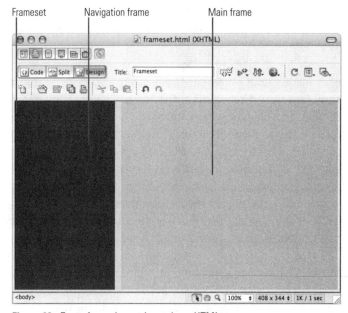

Frameset   Navigation frame   Main frame

Figure 62a Every frame has at least three HTML pages.

What this means is that when you create a frame page, you have to create at least three HTML Web pages. And when you save a frame page, you save at least three HTML pages.

To make this process less confusing, Dreamweaver 8 comes with a very complete set of frameset page designs. These page designs include almost every useful configuration of pages within a frameset. You can view these page designs by choosing File > New, and choosing the Framesets category in the General tab of the New Document dialog (**Figure 62b**).

Designing with Frames

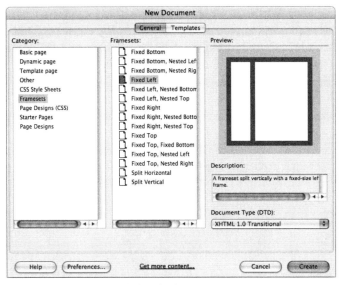

Figure 62b Available page designs for framesets.

After you survey the available frameset designs, choose one from the Framesets column in the New Document dialog and click Create. *All* the required HTML pages will be generated.

After you generate a frameset using one of the available page designs, you can click in any of the embedded pages, and add and edit content just as you would with any Web page. However, you can define unique page attributes for each page within a frameset. For example, different pages within a frameset can have different page background colors, or even have different external style sheets attached to them.

Tip
For an exploration of defining page backgrounds or attaching external style sheets, see Chapter 11, "Formatting Page Elements with CSS."

Making Frames More Accessible

As noted in the introduction to this chapter, frames provide an accessibility challenge for vision-impaired visitors. This is because separating content into more than one page can be confusing when that content is read aloud.

Dreamweaver provides a way to define descriptive page titles for each embedded page. Normally, page titles are not relevant for embedded pages. The title of the container page for the frameset displays in the title bar of a browser, and for non-vision—impaired visitors, it all looks like one page.

On the other hand, page titles for each embedded page are a navigation assistance to vision-impaired visitors. If you select the proper accessibility settings, Dreamweaver will prompt you to define page titles for each embedded page when you generate a frameset. To enable this feature, choose Edit (Windows) or Dreamweaver (Mac) > Preferences. Select the Accessibility category in the Preferences dialog, and check the Frames check box. Click OK in the dialog. After doing this, you'll be prompted to add page titles to embedded pages in framesets.

#63 Examining and Formatting Framesets and Frame Attributes

Frameset attributes include whether or not to display borders between pages in the frameset, as well as the width and/or height of various frames within the frameset. Both these attributes are defined in the Property Inspector. The tricky part is selecting the entire frameset to access these features.

The easiest way to select an entire frameset is to view the Frames panel (Window > Frames). Click on the border that surrounds the entire panel to select the frameset (**Figure 63a**).

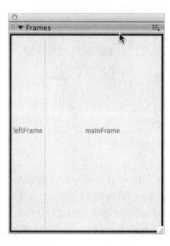

Figure 63a Selecting a frameset in the Frames panel.

Often, framesets are formatted so that there is no visible border between frames in a browser window. The "page" appears to be a single page in a browser, even though it is in fact at least three pages (**Figure 63b**).

Figure 63b What appears to be a single, seamless page in a browser is actually three different HTML Web pages.

Defining Frame Attributes vs. Defining Frameset Attributes

Defining frame attributes is confusing because some attributes are defined for an entire frameset, and other attributes are defined just for a selected frame. And some attributes can be defined for either.

Define border display for your entire frameset. Define the width and/or height for each frame within a frameset as part of defining frameset properties.

Define scroll attributes (whether to display a scrollbar) for a selected frame. Also, define resize permission for a selected frame. You *can* define border parameters for a selected frame that conflict with the settings you define for the entire frameset. Don't! This will confuse browsers.

You determine whether you are defining attributes for a frame or an entire frameset by clicking to select either the entire frameset or an individual frame in the Frames panel.

By default, framesets generated using Dreamweaver's page designs are formatted to display no border between frames. To add a border, choose Yes from the Borders pop-up menu in the Property inspector, and define the border width in pixels in the Border width field. Choose a border color from the Border color swatch (**Figure 63c**).

Figure 63c Defining a border between frames in a frameset.

To define the widths (or heights) of frames within a frameset, use the RowCol Selection area to click a row or column in your frameset. Then, choose a value for the selected column or row in the Column or Row Value field. Values can be either fixed (in pixels), or percent. Or, you can make a column width Relative, which means it will fill all space leftover after columns with fixed widths are displayed (**Figure 63d**).

Figure 63d Defining a frame that will fill all available space after fixed width frames display.

You can define scroll attributes (whether or not to display scroll-bars), as well as setting resize permission (whether or not to allow a viewer to click and drag on the border between frames and resize them in his or her browser) for selected frames.

First, click a specific frame in the Frames panel. The Property inspector then makes settings available for scrollbar display in the Scroll pop-up menu. You can choose Yes (always display a scroll-bar), No (never display a scrollbar), Auto (display a scrollbar only as needed), or Default (whatever a browser defaults to). You can enable viewer resizing of frames by deselecting the No resize check box (**Figure 63e**).

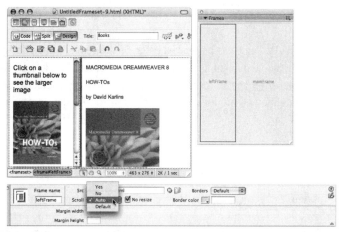

Figure 63e Enabling a scrollbar (only as needed) for a selected frame.

#64 Defining Links Between Frames

Defining links in framesets presents a special challenge. Normally—by default—links open in the same browser window and page that the original link was in. That's a problem in a frameset, because normally you want a link to open in a *different* browser window.

For example, let's examine how this works in a simple, basic, two-frame frameset with a left navigation frame and a right main frame. Links clicked in the left frame *open in the right frame*. The right side of the frameset changes, as new pages open in that frame depending on what link is clicked in the left frame.

This is done by defining a target frame for links. After you define a link for text or an image using the Property inspector (enter the linked page in the Link box), define a target for that link from the Target pop-up menu in the Property inspector.

When you generated a frameset from one of Dreamweaver's frameset page designs, you automatically assigned names to each frame within the frameset. These named frames show up in a list when you click the Target pop-up menu in the Property inspector (**Figure 64a**).

Figure 64a Choosing a target for a link in a frameset.

One More Good Reason to Rely on Dreamweaver Page Designs

When you generate frame-sets using Dreamweaver page designs, each frame is automatically named with a helpful name (like leftFrame or mainFrame). Those frame names are then available in the Target pop-up menu in the Property inspector when you define frame links.

Dreamweaver doesn't do *all* the work for you, however. You still need to remember to define an appropriate frame target for links launched from a frame.

It can be rather disastrous if you don't define the target for a link in a frameset, as when a link doesn't open in the appropriate frame, but in the frame from which the link was launched (**Figure 64b**).

Figure 64b Oops! A link that should have opened in the main frame opened in the left navigation frame.

CHAPTER THIRTEEN

Embedding Media

Media—audio and video files—has always been a dynamic, entertaining, attention-grabbing, and fun element of Web content. Media content has also, historically, been some of the least *accessible* Web content due to long download times and uneven implementation of the plug-ins (software) required to see and hear online media.

As Bob Dylan has said, "the times, they are a-changin'." The steady increase in the availability of high-speed Internet connections (along with improvements in streaming techniques that allow media to begin playing more quickly) means more and more people browsing the Web will enjoy video clips without having to endure an inordinate wait. Surveys and estimates indicate that the vast majority of visitors have appropriate software to watch and hear media in the most widely used formats—Windows Media, Flash, QuickTime, and RealMedia.

Another factor in the widespread acceptance of online video is the increasing number of people who have high-quality sound systems and larger screens and/or screens that display millions of colors.

You can add digital media to your site quickly and easily. This book cannot explore the whole fascinating and wide-ranging scope of software tools and techniques involved in generating video or audio files, but almost every computer shipped these days comes with at least a basic program for editing and producing digital audio and video files you create with your digital video camera, audio recording device, or whatever level of media production tools is available to you.

#65 Linking to Media Files

When I teach digital media for the Web, students are generally shocked at how easy it is to put digital media online and make it available to visitors to your Web site.

The basic steps are:

1. Get the digital media file—make it, have it made for you, buy it, or use available public domain media content.

2. Upload the digital media file to your server using the Dreamweaver Files panel.

3. Create a link to that media file.

It's that simple. I'll walk you through the process in more detail, but first, there are a few issues to explore and for you to make decisions about.

There are accessibility issues connected with including media in your Web site (see sidebar). You might want to make visitors aware of download options for different types of Internet connections (**Figure 65a**).

Accessibility Issues for Web Media

Consider accessibility issues when you post online media content. Large media files take a long time to download—especially if your visitors are using dial-up connections. Online media also requires necessary software. QuickTime audio and video files require the QuickTime Player (a free dowload, available at www.quicktime.com). By default, QuickTime Player is not installed on many Windows computers. RealMedia files require a downloadable media player as well—you can find a free version of RealPlayer at www.real.com.

Flash files require the Flash Player, which is installed on a large percentage of computers, and is also available as a free download. Windows Media files play seamlessly on Windows machines, but Mac users may need to download the Mac version of the player. In short, most media files require *plug-in* software—software that adds features to your browser. You should make it easy for visitors to your site to download that software if they need it.

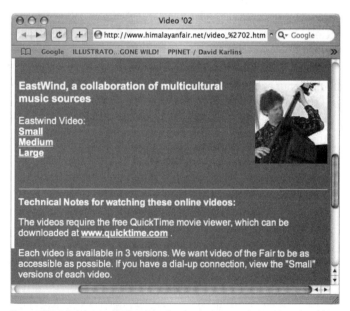

Figure 65a A link is provided to download software needed to view the video, and different download options are provided for different connection speeds.

If possible, it's best to prepare three versions of your media files—one highest-quality for high-speed download, one medium-quality, and one low-quality (and thus a smaller file) for dial-up downloading.

Once you have prepared one or more files for download, follow theses steps to make the files available for download:

1. Copy the files into the folder you use for your Dreamweaver Web site.

2. Enter text or place an image that will serve as a link, and select that text or image.

3. In the Property inspector, use the Link icon to create a link from the text or image to the media file (**Figure 65b**).

Figure 65b Defining a link from text to a Windows Media (AVI) file.

Tip

You will often want to open a media file in a new browser window. This way, when a visitor is done viewing (or listening to) the file, he or she can close the browser window playing the media file, and return to the original page. Do this by choosing _blank in the Target pop-up menu in the Property inspector right after you define the link to your media file.

Digital Media Files Are Large

Digital media can take very large amounts of space on your server. If you contracted for a small Web site and you want to add media files, you might have to contact your Web host provider, and tell them that you are going to be uploading large media files. Look over your Web hosting agreement, see how much data is allowed on your site, and then total the file sizes of your media files to make sure you have arranged for sufficient server space.

#66 Creating Flash Text in Dreamweaver

Flash Text vs. FlashPaper

Flash Text cannot be copied and pasted, nor can it be searched. It is essentially a media object. There is a component of the Macromedia Studio 8 Suite that does create Flash Text that can be copied and pasted in a browser by visitors, and is searchable. FlashPaper is bundled with Studio 8, and the FlashPaper documents it generates are copy and pasteable, as well as searchable. If you have Studio 8 with FlashPaper, you can print documents to FlashPaper format from programs like Microsoft Word in OS X or in Windows XP. FlashPaper works as a distinct open application window into which you can copy (and then save) text.

After creating a FlashPaper document, you embed it in a Dreamweaver document by choosing Insert > Media > FlashPaper, and then navigating to and choosing a FlashPaper file using the Insert FlashPaper dialog. For more on using FlashPaper objects in Dreamweaver, see #72 later in this chapter.

Flash Text looks like type, but technically it is media in the sense that it is a graphical media file that requires a media player (the Flash Player).

Flash Text opens a whole other dimension of what is possible with text on the Web. As discussed in Chapter 8, "Formatting Text," the introduction of Cascading Style Sheets (CSS) opened the door to formatting features such as line spacing, relatively precise font-size controls, and background color. But CSS does not solve the problem of displaying actual fonts. Even with CSS, font display is dependent on the fonts installed on a visitor's system. So, if you use Palatino font and your visitor's computer does not have Palatino installed, he or she will not see the text in Palatino font, and instead the text will display as Times Roman or another font.

Flash Text allows you to create text using any font available on your system, and to display that font online, regardless of what fonts are installed on your visitor's system (**Figure 66a**).

Figure 66a The Flash Text page banner appears with the assigned font regardless of what fonts are installed on a visitor's system.

You generate Flash Text right in Dreamweaver, and the object you create is saved as a Flash movie in the Flash SWF file format. Since Flash Text is, essentially, an embedded Flash movie, Dreamweaver has to generate HTML code that embeds a Flash file. In order for the link to work and not get corrupted, Dreamweaver has to know the file name of the HTML document you are working on. Therefore (and here's the point), save your page before generating and embedding a Flash Text object.

Once you've saved the page into which the Flash Text will be embedded, follow these steps to generate and embed Flash Text:

1. With your cursor at the point where you want to insert the Flash Text, choose Insert > Media > Flash Text. The Insert Flash Text dialog will open. Select the Show font check box to activate the preview feature that displays the actual font you select in the Text field of the dialog.

2. In the Text field (**Figure 66b**), enter the text you want to appear on your page as Flash Text.

Figure 66b Previewing Flash Text as you generate it in the Insert Flash Text dialog.

3. From the Font pop-up menu, choose a font. In the Size field, enter text size in points.

4. Use the Bold, Italic, and the Left-, Center-, or Right-align icons under the Font pop-up menu to assign style and alignment to the text.

continued on next page

#66: Creating Flash Text in Dreamweaver

5. From the Color pop-up menu, choose a color, or enter a hexadecimal color value in the Color field. If you want the text color to change when a visitor rolls his or her cursor over it, enter a Rollover color by using the Rollover color pop-up menu or entering a hexadecimal color value in the Rollover color field.

6. If your Flash text is linked to another page or file, enter the link in the Link field. With the Target pop-up menu, you can change the target browser window for the link from the default (opens in the same browser window) to _blank (opens in a new browser window).

7. Choose an optional background color from the Bg color pop-up menu, or enter a hexadecimal color value in the Bg color field.

8. In the Save as field, Dreamweaver automatically generates a filename with a SWF file extension. You can accept that filename, or enter a new one.

Tip

The filename you assign must be unique—that is, there must not be any other file with that name.

9. After you have defined your Flash Text, you can click the Apply button to see how it looks on the page. When the text looks the way you want it to, click OK.

Tip

Depending on your accessibility settings (defined in the Accessibility category of the Preferences dialog—accessed by choosing Edit > Preferences (Windows) or Dreamweaver > Preferences (Mac)—you might get prompted to add accessibility options for Flash Text after you OK the Insert Flash Text dialog. Assigning a Title to the Flash Text object allows reader software to read that content out loud.

You can edit the appearance of Flash Text objects by selecting them and choosing formatting features from the Property inspector, or you can edit the content of Flash Text objects by clicking the Edit button in the Property inspector (**Figure 66c**).

The Property inspector has a couple formatting options that are not available in the Insert Flash Text dialog. Use the V Space field to define vertical spacing between the Flash Text and objects above or below it. Use the H Space field to set horizontal spacing. The Quality pop-up menu allows you to convert the Flash file to a lower-quality, faster-loading file.

Figure 66c The Property inspector with a Flash Text object selected.

#67 Creating Flash Buttons in Dreamweaver

Like Flash Text, Flash buttons are small Flash objects generated in Dreamweaver, and saved to the Flash Player format (SWF). And, like Flash Text, Flash buttons display any font and font size, regardless of browser or system settings (provided the viewer has the Flash Player installed on his or her system).

There are more important similarities between Flash Text and Flash buttons. A Flash button (like Flash Text) can be defined as a link, can have a defined link target, and can have a defined background color (**Figure 67a**).

Figure 67a A set of Flash buttons on a Web page.

The difference between Dreamweaver's Flash Text and Flash buttons is that Flash buttons include graphic designs available through dozens of included Flash button styles and more styles that can be downloaded from the Adobe Dreamweaver Exchange.

Each Flash button is a unique Flash (SWF) file. And in order for Dreamweaver to generate a file in the correct folder, with appropriate links to appear in the page, you have to first save the Dreamweaver Web page *before* inserting Flash buttons. Once you do this, follow these steps to generate and embed Flash buttons:

1. With your cursor at the point where you want to insert the Flash button, choose Insert > Media > Flash Button. The Insert Flash Button dialog will open (**Figure 67b**). As you design the button, a preview of it will appear in the Sample field at the top of the dialog.

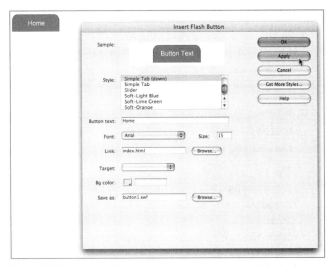

Figure 67b Previewing Flash button text as you generate it in the Insert Flash Button dialog.

2. In the Style field, choose a design for your button from the list.

3. In the Button Text field, enter the text you want to appear in your Flash button.

4. From the Font pop-up menu, choose a font. In the size field, enter text size in points.

5. Normally Flash buttons function as navigation buttons. Use the Link field or the Browse button to define a link.

Tip

See #25, "Defining Links and Link Attributes," for a full explanation of links and how to define them.

continued on next page

#67: Creating Flash Buttons in Dreamweaver

Downloading More Flash Button Styles

There are several sets of additional Flash buttons for sale, or free, at the Adobe Dreamweaver Exchange. Click the Get More Styles button in the Insert Flash Button dialog to open the Adobe Dreamweaver Exchange in your browser (you must be online to do this). The Dreamweaver Exchange was not the most accessible site in the world in the Macromedia era, and at current writing, it's a bit more confusing now that it is being integrated into adobe.com. But persevere. You'll register with Adobe if you have not done so already, and then you can search exchanges for Flash buttons. You'll be prompted to download the Flash button extension that you choose, and then your computer will prompt you to install that extension and restart Dreamweaver. When you do this, you'll see additional Flash button styles available in the Insert Flash Button dialog.

6. Use the Target pop-up menu if you want to change the target browser window for the defined link from the default (opens in the same browser window) to _blank (opens in a new browser window).

7. Choose an optional background color from the BG color pop-up menu, or enter a hexadecimal color value in the BG color field.

8. In the Save as field, Dreamweaver automatically generates a filename with a SWF file extension. You can accept that file name or enter a new one. There's no good reason to change the default button file name.

9. After you have defined your Flash button, click the Apply button to see how it looks on the page. When the text looks the way you want it to, click OK.

Tip

Depending on your accessibility settings (defined in the Accessibility category of the Preferences dialog—accessed by choosing Edit > Preferences (Windows) or Dreamweaver > Preferences (Mac)—Dreamweaver might display the Flash Accessibility Attributes dialog each time you create a Flash button. Assigning a Title to a Flash button allows reader software to read that content aloud.

You can edit the appearance of Flash button objects by selecting them and choosing formatting features from the Property inspector, or you can edit the content of a Flash button by clicking the Edit button in the Property inspector.

Use the V Space field to define vertical spacing between the Flash buttons and objects above or below them. Use the H Space field to set horizontal spacing. The Quality pop-up menu allows you to convert the Flash file to a lower-quality, faster-loading file.

#68 Embedding Flash and Flash Video Files

When you embed a Flash file or a Flash Video file in a Web page in Dreamweaver, you can adjust the size of the movie, define the size and color of a background behind the movie, and even adjust features like whether or not the movie plays automatically when the page in which it is embedded opens, or if a visitor has to click a Play button to watch the movie.

Despite the similar sounding names, Flash movies (SWF files) and Flash Video (FLV files) are different things. Flash movies, often referred to as SWFs, present animated and interactive content online, created with Adobe's Flash authoring tool. The SWF format is also sometimes used to display digital artwork online.

Flash *Video* is a format for sharing movies online, similar to QuickTime, Windows Media, or RealMedia movies.

In this How-To, I'll show you how to embed both SWF files (Flash movies), and Flash Video in a Web page.

When you embed a Flash movie (a SWF file) in a Web page, the movie appears as a gray box. When selected, the Property inspector for the movie is active (**Figure 68a**).

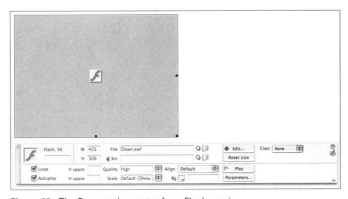

Figure 68a The Property inspector for a Flash movie.

Use the Loop and AutoPlay checkboxes to enable (or disable) looping (repeating) or autoplay (the animation plays when a page is loaded).

The V Space and H Space fields allow you to define vertical (V) or horizontal (H) spacing between the Flash movie and other objects on the page.

The Quality pop-up menu allows you to compress the Flash file (choose Low) for faster downloading and lower quality.

In the Scale pop-up menu, the Default setting maintains the original height-to-width ratio of the original animation (that is, it prevents the animation from being distorted) when the Flash object is resized. The Exact Fit option in the Scale pop-up menu, on the other hand, allows you to stretch the animation horizontally or vertically if you change the original height and/or width.

The Align pop-up menu can be used to align the Flash object left or right, so text flows around the animation (**Figure 68b**).

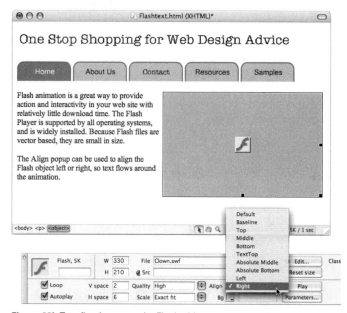

Figure 68b Text flowing around a Flash object.

The Bg pop-up menu can be used to define a background color. The background color is active if you resize the Flash object and maintain the height-to-width aspect ratio by choosing the Default setting in the Scale field.

The Reset size button restores the Flash object to its original size. The Edit button opens Flash (if you have it installed) to edit the Flash object.

The Play button displays the Flash object in the Document window. Toggling to Stop displays the editable gray box (**Figure 68c**).

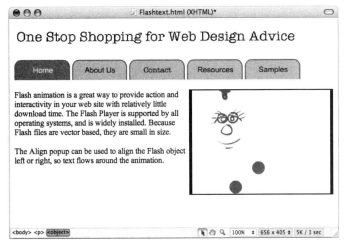

Figure 68c Playing a Flash animation in the Document window.

Dreamweaver 8 allows you to embed movies that have been saved to the Flash Video format (FLV), and then choose from a nice little set of player controls that display in a browser window to make it easy for visitors to control the movie.

To embed a Flash Video file, follow these steps:

1. Choose Insert > Media > Flash Video. The Insert Flash Video dialog will open (**Figure 68d**). Use the Browse button to navigate to a Flash Video (FLV) file (or enter the URL of a file on the Internet) in the URL field. Unless you are working with a special streaming server (and your server administration will know this information), choose Progressive Download Video from the Video Type pop-up menu.

continued on next page

Flash Files vs. Flash Video

The Flash file format (SWF, often pronounced "swiff") is a long-established format for presenting animation and interactivity online. Flash files are often used for animated ads or interactive forms. The SWF format is the only Web-friendly format that supports vector graphics—graphics that can be enlarged in a browser without distorting the artwork. Complex Flash files can be as engaging and sophisticated as video games. The SWF format is actually the file formatted by the Flash Player, while editable Flash files are saved to FLA format.

Flash Video (FLV) files are different. Adobe is promoting the FLV format as a kind of "universal" video format that transcends other competing media formats. Flash 8 includes a utility that converts files from Windows Media, QuickTime, and other formats to Flash Video (FLV). The Flash Video (FLV) format is used, for example, as the video format central to the popularity of youtube.com.

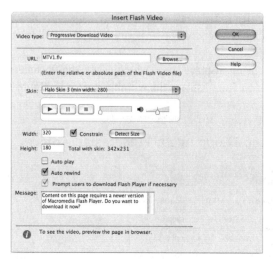

Figure 68d Embedding a Flash Video file.

2. Click the Detect Size button in the dialog to detect the size of the video. Keep the Constrain check box selected since it is unlikely that you will want to distort the height-to-width ratio of the video. You can enter a new value in either the Width or Height field to resize the video (if you selected the Constrain check box, the nonedited dimension will automatically adjust to keep the height-to-width ratio of the video the same as the original).

3. After detecting the video size, you can use the Skin pop-up menu to select a player control set. Note that player controls require various sizes of videos (that's why you detected the video size in step 2 first).

4. You can enable the Auto play, Auto rewind, or Prompt users to download Flash Player features if necessary using the check boxes in the dialog. If you elect to prompt users to download the Flash Player, you can accept or edit the text message that displays.

Many Flash Video parameters you set when you embed the video can be edited in the Property inspector.

#69 Embedding QuickTime Media

QuickTime movies can be easily embedded in Dreamweaver pages. And you can easily reset the size at which QuickTime movies will display as. However, Dreamweaver does not provide easy-to-use sets of controllers for QuickTime movies like it does for Flash Video. Features like background color, autoplay, and scale (enlargement of a video by displaying it at a lower resolution) are all defined with parameters that have to be entered manually.

To embed a QuickTime movie, choose Insert > Media > Plugin. The all-purpose Select File dialog (that is used for all types of plug-ins, not just QuickTime files) will open. Navigate to the QuickTime (MOV) file you wish to insert, and click Choose (Mac) or OK (Windows).

The embedded QuickTime movie appears as a very minimalist 32-pixel square box, regardless of the size of the actual movie. To display the movie at an appropriate size, enter a height and width in the Property inspector. You can also enter vertical (V) or horizontal (H) spacing in the Property inspector. The Align pop-up menu can be used to align the movie on the left or right side of the page (**Figure 69a**).

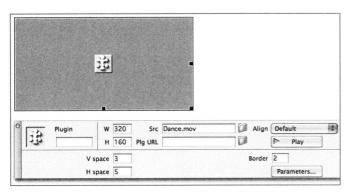

Figure 69a Defining parameters for an embedded QuickTime movie.

You can try to preview QuickTime movies in Dreamweaver by clicking the Play button in the Property inspector. Support for this feature is spotty in Dreamweaver 8, so instead, rely on previewing the movie in a browser (choose File > Preview in Browser, and select a browser from the available list if you have more than one) (**Figure 69b**).

Figure 69b Testing a QuickTime movie in a browser.

As noted, Dreamweaver does not have built-in features for defining basic display parameters for QuickTime movies. Instead, you manually enter those parameters into the Parameter section of the Property inspector. Click the Parameters button in the Property inspector to display the Parameters dialog. You can add parameters by clicking the "+" symbol in the dialog. Enter a parameter by entering it in the left column, and enter a value in the right column.

Following are a few useful parameters for controlling the display of QuickTime movies:

- The BGCOLOR parameter defines the background color. Enter standard colors (like red, blue, green, black) or hexadecimal color values.

- The SCALE parameter enlarges a video by making the resolution more grainy. Setting scale value to 2, for example, doubles the size of the video display without affecting the number of pixels.

- The autoplay parameter can be set to true (the video plays when the page opens) or false.

- The volume parameter defines the default volume for the video when it plays on a scale of 1 (quiet) to 10 (loud).

After you set parameters, click OK to close the Parameters dialog (**Figure 69c**).

Find More QuickTime Parameters

Parameters for embedding QuickTime movies can be found at http://www.apple.com/quicktime/tutorials/embed.html.

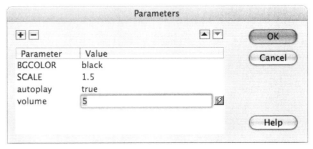

Figure 69c Defining background color, scale, autoplay, and volume preset for a QuickTime movie.

As noted earlier, you can preview your QuickTime movie in the Dreamweaver Document window, but you'll have more reliable preview results if you preview the page with the movie in a Web browser.

#**69**: Embedding QuickTime Media

#70 Embedding Windows Media

Like QuickTime movies, Windows Media files (which can be WMV, AVI, and other file types) can be easily embedded in Dreamweaver. And you can easily reset the size at which Windows Media movies will display. As with QuickTime movies, Dreamweaver does not provide easy-to-use sets of controllers for Windows Media movies. And, as with QuickTime movies, you need to manually define parameters to control features like autoplay, initial volume, and whether or not a player control displays in the browser with the video.

To embed a Windows Media movie, choose Insert > Media > Plugin. The Select File dialog (used for all types of plug-ins) opens. Navigate to the Windows Media file you wish to insert, and click Choose (Mac) or OK (Windows).

The embedded Windows Media movie is placed on the page in a 32-pixel square box, regardless of the size of the actual movie. To display the movie at an appropriate size, enter a width and height in the Property inspector. You can also enter vertical (V) or horizontal (H) spacing in the Property inspector. The Align pop-up menu can be used to align the movie on the left or right side of the page (**Figure 70a**).

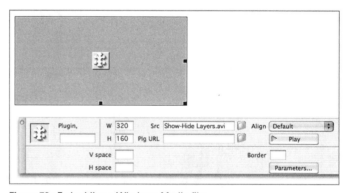

Figure 70a Embedding a Windows Media file.

The best way to see how your Windows Media file will look in a browser is to preview the movie in a browser (choose File > Preview in Browser, and select a browser from the available list if you have more than one).

To define how the Windows Media file displays and plays in a browser, you enter parameters into the Parameter area of the Property inspector. Click the Parameters button in the Property inspector to display the Parameters dialog. You can add parameters by clicking the "+" symbol in the dialog. Enter a parameter in the left column, and enter a value in the right column.

Following are a few useful parameters for controlling the display of Windows Media movies:

- The autostart parameter with the Value set to true plays a movie automatically when the page opens. When the value is set to false, it does not, and requires the visitor start the movie using a control.

- The displaybackcolor parameter can have the Value set to false (no background color) or a color (like red, blue, green, or black) or a hexadecimal value.

- The ShowAudioControls can have the Value set to true (a volume control displays) or false (no control).

After you set parameters, click OK to close the Parameters dialog (**Figure 70b**).

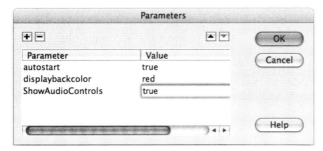

Figure 70b Parameters for a Windows Media movie.

Where Do You Find Windows Media Parameters?

There are many versions of Windows Media Player, and they use different parameters. While QuickTime parameters are standardized and managed by Apple, the world of Windows Media is less defined. You can Google for Windows Media parameters, but you'll have to sort through competing and conflicting sets of parameters. The bottom line is that Windows Media video will display in a visitor's browser window in unpredictable ways. While Windows Media is almost universally supported, developers who need tight control over the display of embedded video turn to Flash video, Real video, or QuickTime.

#71 Embedding RealMedia

Dreamweaver supports Flash files (SWF) and Flash Video files (FLV) with easy-to-use, built-in formatting features, and does not support Windows Media or QuickTime video at all (you have to enter parameters manually in the Property inspector to format these video file formats). RealMedia files (including RM and RAM) are also not supported by Dreamweaver very well, but there is a downloadable extension available from Adobe that makes it easy to define Real video parameters without resorting to looking them up and entering them manually.

If you're going to be working with Real video, download that extension. You'll find it at the Dreamweaver Exchange at Adobe. com. Search the exchange for "realmedia," and the one result will be the RealMedia extension. Follow instructions at the exchange to download and install the extension.

At this writing, Adobe has Studio 8 exchanges at www.adobe. com/cfusion/exchange/. Otherwise, search the Adobe site for Dreamweaver extensions.

The RealMedia extension is an oldie but goodie. Developed in 2001 by David Warner, it remains a useful tool for embedding Real video (or audio) into Dreamweaver-created Web pages, and is the only bridge accessible to noncoders between Real video and Dreamweaver. The RealMedia extension creates something called a *metafile* that is necessary for the media file to play, along with generating JavaScript that controls the RealMedia file.

Real Player—The Bad Boy of Digital Media

RealMedia, the company that supplies the RealPlayer and owns the RealMedia format, has a reputation for being difficult to access. That's certainly the case for Mac users. You cannot embed RealMedia files in a Web page and have them play in a browser supported by OSX (you can open RealMedia files in Real-Player, outside of a Web page). And even in Windows, Real-Player has some drawbacks—it's much more of a hassle to download than other players. That's because Real has a different financial model than QuickTime, Windows Media, or Flash. Real puts more emphasis on selling it's pay-to-use player, and so viewers who want to quickly download the free version of the player often have a hard time finding it at the Real site.

So why put up with RealMedia? RealMedia has the most effective streaming technology, allowing RealMedia videos to start playing quickly. And the Real-Player can be very precisely configured in complex Web sites, providing an unmatched set of controls and information display.

To embed and configure a RealMedia video in Dreamweaver 8 for Windows, with the RealMedia extension installed, follow these steps:

1. In Dreamweaver 8, you can access the RealMedia extension through the Insert bar. Choose Insert from the Window menu to display the Insert bar, and choose RealAudio from the list of categories (on the left side of the Insert bar) (**Figure 71a**).

Figure 71a Embedding a RealAudio file.

2. In the RealMedia Insert bar, click the RealVideo button. The Select File dialog will open. Navigate to a Real video file and click OK. The video appears in your document with a Real icon, and the Property inspector displays the filename plus a few other options (**Figure 71b**).

Figure 71b An embedded Real video.

continued on next page

#71: Embedding RealMedia

3. In the Property inspector, with the Real video icon selected, set the width in the W field and the Height in the H field (both dimensions should be set in pixels).

4. If you wish to have the video launch when the page is opened, select the Auto-Start check box.

5. To add a control panel (so viewers can start, stop, pause, and adjust volume), click the RealMedia control button in the RealAudio dialog. The RealMedia Control dialog will appear with a single pop-up menu. From the Control pop-up menu, select a control element. The Basic Control is a good, all-purpose combination of useful controls (**Figure 71c**).

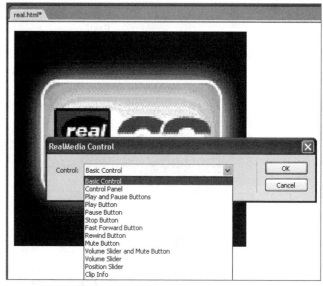

Figure 71c Choosing a control for a RealMedia file.

6. Click OK in the RealMedia Control dialog to insert the control panel. It will appear in the Document window below your video (**Figure 71d**).

Figure 71d A control panel for a Real video.

continued on next page

#71: Embedding RealMedia

7. You can test your embedded video by choosing File > Preview in Browser, and choosing Internet Explorer—an environment that supports embedded RealMedia content (**Figure 71e**).

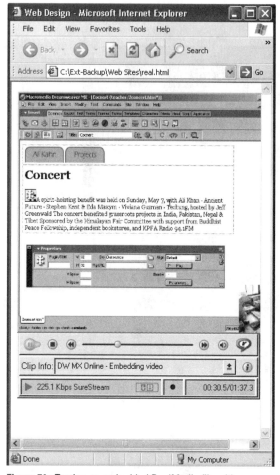

Figure 71e Testing an embedded RealMedia file with a control panel.

After you embed your RealMedia video file, save and upload both the Web page and the video file. *Do* choose to upload dependent files, as the RealMedia extension generates a real.rpm file necessary to display the video.

#72 Including FlashPaper and PDF Files on Your Site

FlashPaper and PDF documents solve the age-old (or cyber-age–old) problem of how to actually control the layout of an online document. When you create HTML pages, you are at the mercy of the display environment. Windows or Mac? Linux? A large monitor or handheld device? A full set of installed fonts?

FlashPaper and PDF documents solve these problems. They create files that look the same in print or online.

Traditionally, Web designers have not embedded PDF pages within HTML pages. This is not something that is easy to do, or that works smoothly in browsers. Adobe, however, has posed the possibility of embedding FlashPaper documents right in a Web page. Promotional materials for FlashPaper, as well as features in Dreamweaver, make it easy and encourage it. So technically it is an accessible option. And, based on my experimentation, there is a case that embedded FlashPaper documents might be something users find helpful. The documents are completely scalable, so readers can easily enlarge type for accessibility reasons. The text can be copied into a word processor document. And visitors to Web sites can easily access the FlashPaper document. Rather than launch the document in a separate window, they simply follow a link to an HTML Web page and seamlessly interact with the FlashPaper or PDF document.

Since FlashPaper documents are saved to the same SWF format as regular Flash objects, they are easy to embed and format in Dreamweaver.

To embed a FlashPaper document in an open Web page (in the Dreamweaver Document window), follow these steps:

1. Choose Insert > Media > FlashPaper. The Insert FlashPaper dialog will appear.

continued on next page

FlashPaper vs. PDF

PDF and FlashPaper documents both preserve formatting and layout that is not normally protected when documents are shared. The PDF format is much more robust and developed, and has options for things like signable forms that are not available in FlashPaper. However, FlashPaper documents can be much more easily and smoothly embedded right in a Web page.

2. Use the Browse button to navigate to and select a FlashPaper file, or enter a URL of a file on the Internet in the Source field. Enter a height and width for the embedded FlashPaper document. Click OK to embed the FlashPaper document (**Figure 72a**).

Figure 72a Choosing and sizing a FlashPaper file to embed.

3. With the FlashPaper document selected, the Property inspector displays formatting options for Flash objects. Some features applicable to animation (like autoplay or loop) are inoperative and not relevant. But you can right- or left-align the document relative to the text using the Align pop-up menu. You can define vertical (V) or horizontal (H) spacing as a buffer between the FlashPaper document and other content, and you can rescale width (W) or height (H) (**Figure 72b**).

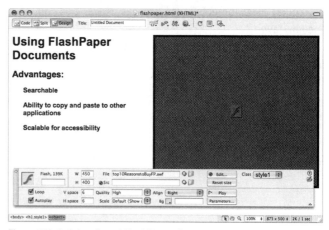

Figure 72b A right-aligned FlashPaper document with 6 pixels of vertical and horizontal spacing.

CHAPTER FOURTEEN

Collecting Data in Forms

Forms provide a uniquely interactive element in a Web site. Through a form, you not only *convey* content, you *collect* content. This content can range from orders for products, feedback on site content, service requests and subscription list sign-ups, to surveys, forum discussions, and opinion polls.

Some form content is managed using scripts that run in the visitor's browser. Such scripts are referred to as *client-side* data handling. Other forms collect data and send it to a server, where scripts on the server manage the data. These are called *server-side* forms. Most form data is managed by server-side scripts. One example of a server-side script is a mailing list form. Visitors enter information (at least an email address, and maybe more) into a form. That data is then stored in a database on a remote server. It can be accessed to send out mailings.

In short, this chapter explains how to design two kinds of forms:

- Forms that manage data in the browser (client-side).

- Forms that connect to scripts at a server (server-side)

In this chapter, you will learn how to connect a form to an existing server script (but not how to program the scripts), and I'll throw in some tips on where you can find already packaged server scripts to handle things like search forms, sign-up mailing lists, and discussion forums.

#73 Creating Jump Menus

One great example of a client-side form is a jump menu—where a visitor selects a page in your Web site from a pop-up menu. A jump menu works because script (in this case using JavaScript) acts on a form and effects an action (in this case opening a new Web page) based on data the visitor entered into the form (the page he or she chose from the jump menu). Dreamweaver creates jump menu forms and automatically generates the required JavaScript.

Jump menus are an efficient and attractive way to allow visitors to navigate your site. You can provide a long list of target links in a jump menu without using much valuable space on your Web page (**Figure 73a**).

Figure 73a Providing a long list of navigation options in a jump menu.

Jump menus use JavaScript to handle form input. In other words, when a visitor chooses a Web page (or other link, like an image file) from the jump menu, Dreamweaver generates JavaScript code to open the selected page in a browser window. You don't need to worry about this JavaScript. But you can look at it in Code view in the Document window if you're interested in seeing what the JavaScript looks like (or, if you know how to, you can edit the generated JavaScript in Code view of the Document window).

To create a jump menu, follow these steps:

1. With a page open in the Document window, choose Insert > Form > Jump Menu. The Insert Jump Menu dialog will open.

2. In the Text field of the Insert Jump Menu dialog, enter the text that will appear in the jump menu.

   Note
   The text you enter in the Text field defines the name of the menu item; you don't have to enter it separately.

3. In the When Selected, Go to URL field, either enter a URL for a link, or use the Browse button to navigate to and select a file on your site (**Figure 73b**).

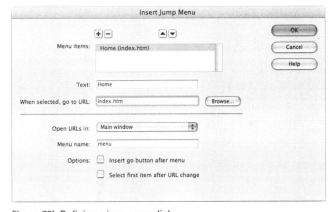

Figure 73b Defining a jump menu link.

continued on next page

#73: Creating Jump Menus

Details of Defining a Jump Menu

In the Insert Jump Menu dialog, the Open URLs in field allows you to define a frame in which to open a linked page. It applies only if you are working in frames (see Chapter 12, "Designing with Frames" for a full discussion of frames). The Menu name field is automatically filled out by Dreamweaver and enables Dreamweaver to generate JavaScript to manage the input. In the Options area of the dialog, the Insert go button after menu check box generates a "Go" button for your jump menu. The Go button is not reliably supported by browsers and should be avoided. The Select first item after URL change check box automatically places the first jump menu option as the selected choice after the jump menu is used to navigate to a page.

4. Define additional jump menu options by clicking the "+" button in the dialog, and entering new text and URL. Repeat to enter as many jump menu options as you need. Delete an item from the jump menu by selecting it and clicking the "–" button.

5. To change the order of an item in the jump menu list, select the item and use the Up and Down arrow buttons in the dialog to move the selected item up or down in the list (**Figure 73c**).

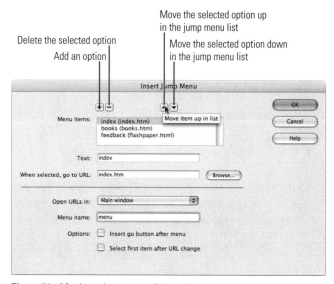

Figure 73c Moving a jump menu link up in the list of options.

6. After you define all the links in the jump menu, click OK to generate the menu. Test the menu in a browser (you can't test it in the Dreamweaver Document window because the jump menu works with JavaScript in a browser).

To edit an existing jump menu, you need to open the Behavior that Dreamweaver created to control the jump menu. View the Behaviors panel (choose Window > Behaviors). Click the jump menu to select it. As you do, you will see Jump Menu listed in the second column of the Behaviors panel. Double-click it to reopen the Jump Menu dialog and edit the jump menu (**Figure 73d**).

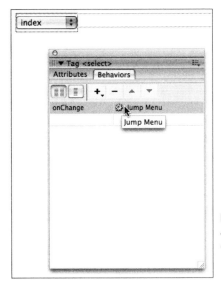

Figure 73d Opening the Jump Menu dialog by double-clicking Jump Menu in the Behaviors panel.

The Jump Menu dialog looks just like the Insert Jump Menu dialog, and you can add, remove, or move menu items or change menu options in this dialog.

#74 Embedding Forms Linked to Server Databases

Server-Side Script Developer Resource

Setting up a server database and generating scripts on it to manage data is beyond the scope of this book, but is covered in detail in *Macromedia Dreamweaver 8 Advanced for Windows and Macintosh: Visual QuickPro Guide,* by Lucinda Dykes (Peachpit Press, 2006).

There are many online services that provide you with server-side databases and scripts, and these services often host online databases and scripts as well (or else they tell you how to copy them to your server). For example, there are services that allow you to host a mailing list at their server. They provide you with HTML that you copy into your Web page. That HTML contains the coding for the form, as well as a connection to a script at a server that manages data put into the form.

One of the most popular, easy to use, reliable, and professional online form-and-script services is the Freefind search engine service. Freefind will index your site (compile a list of all words in your site in a database), and provide you with a form that visitors can enter search criteria into.

You can find online database and script services by searching for "CGI scripts." CGI stands for *common gateway interface* and is the protocol (system) that is used (with options for various programming languages) to manage form input.

Follow these steps to place a Freefind search field on an open Dreamweaver Web page. You can also use them as a model for using similar services.

1. Go to freefind.com, and enter your email address and your site's URL. Click the Instant Signup button. Freefind will email you a password and login and a link to the Freefind control center. Follow the link, log in, and clink the link for a free search field (or you can choose one of the more elaborate, ad-free, pay options).

2. Click the Build Index tab in the Freefind control center, and then click the Index Now link. Freefind will build a database, at the Freefind server, of all the words in your Web site.

3. Click the HTML tab and choose one of the four available types of search field forms you can use (the options are Site Search Only, Site and Web Search, Web Search Only, or Text Links).

4. Select all the HTML for the search field you selected, and chose Edit > Copy from your browser menu.

5. Back in Dreamweaver, click in the Document window to set the place where the search field will be inserted. Then choose View > Code to switch to code view. Don't worry about any of the code you see—your cursor is in the spot you clicked in Design view. Choose Edit > Paste to place the HTML code, and switch back to Design view to see the search field (**Figure 74**).

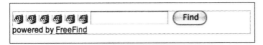

Figure 74 Placing a search field from Freefind.

Test your search field in a browser. The search field form has fields and buttons. You can reformat the fields and buttons using the techniques for defining form and form field attributes covered in the rest of this chapter. In other words, you can customize the way this form looks—you just can't delete any of the form fields. Further techniques in this chapter will cover how customization works, so you can customize forms you get from CGI hosts.

Helpful CGI Scripts, Forms, and Hosting Services

In addition to the Freefind search service, there are a few other useful sources for scripts and hosting to manage form data. These sites provide various sets of available forms and scripts that collect Web statistics, collect feedback, manage message boards, generate survey polls, allow guestbook listings, and store and manage email lists.

- www.thefreecountry.com
- www.cgispy.com
- www.sitegadgets.com
- cgi.resourceindex.com

#75 Defining a Form in Dreamweaver

Normally, forms display in the Document window (in Design view) as dashed red lines. This border is invisible in a browser. Dreamweaver displays the borders of forms as a highly helpful tool so that you can make sure all your form fields are inside your form. If they're not inside the form, they won't work.

Displaying form outlines is a default option that can be turned off. If you don't see the dashed red line indicating the form, turn on this option by choosing View > Visual Aids > Invisible Elements. With Invisible Elements selected in this submenu, you'll be able to see your form.

Form data is collected using different kinds of form fields. Text is entered into text boxes or text areas. Options can be selected from sets of radio (option) buttons. Data can be uploaded using file fields. And forms are submitted (or cleared) using submit (or clear) buttons.

None of these form fields, however, works without a *form*. It's important to be conscious of this. Many of my students get frustrated trying to figure out why their sets of form fields aren't doing anything when the problem is that those form fields are not embedded inside a form.

Further, a page can have more than one form. That's often not a good idea from a design standpoint, but there are imaginable situations when you might give visitors a choice of different forms to fill out.

To create a form in an open Web page in Dreamweaver, simply click to place the location of the form, and choose Insert > Form > Form. The form will display as a dashed red box. The Property inspector displays the form name.

Make sure you have clicked *inside the form* before you add any form fields! (**Figure 75a**)

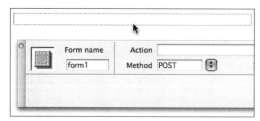

Figure 75a A form placed on a page in Dreamweaver.

Forms can be a big hassle for visitors with disabilities. Form accessibility issues include making it easy for disabled visitors (who, for example, cannot use a mouse) to move from field to field in a form, and to easily select form fields. Dreamweaver 8 promotes accessibility in many ways, including form design. If you activate accessibility prompts for form design, Dreamweaver will prompt you to enter accessibility features for each form field as you place it in the form.

To activate prompts for accessibility options in forms, choose Edit (Windows) or Dreamweaver (Mac) > Preferences, and select the Accessibility category. Select the Form objects check box if it is not already selected (**Figure 75b**).

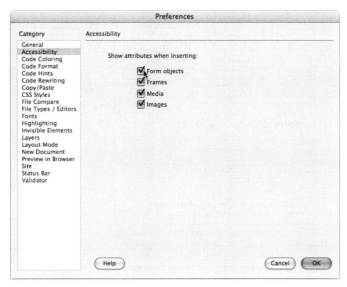

Figure 75b Activating prompts for accessibility options when designing forms.

With form accessibility options activated, Dreamweaver will prompt you with the Input Tag Accessibility Attributes dialog when you insert a form field into a form. The accessibility options allow for visitors to fill out the form without using a mouse, or if they are relying on reader software, to have an identifying label read to them.

#75: Defining a Form in Dreamweaver

You can enter a label in the Label field in the Input Tag Accessibility Attributes dialog, and use the radio buttons in the Style and Position areas to format and position the tag (**Figure 75a**). In the Access key field, you can enter a key (normally a letter) that visitors can use to select that field. For example, you might assign the letter *N* to a "Name" field. In the Tab Index field, enter a numerical value to define the order in which visitors will tab to the defined field when they use their tab key to navigate between fields. Tab Indexes and Access keys are used by visitors who cannot use a mouse.

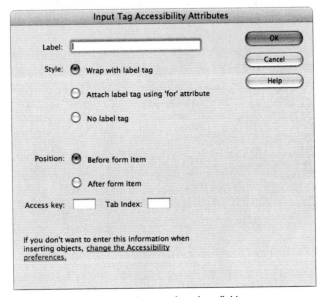

Figure 75c Defining access features for a form field.

#76 Placing Text Fields and Text Areas

Text fields are the most widely used way of collecting data. Email addresses, phone numbers, purchase prices, zip codes, names, and a wide variety of other data are collected in text fields.

Text fields collect a single line of text. Text areas can collect multiple lines of text. Text areas are used to collect comments, descriptions (like descriptions of problems for online service forms), guestbook entries, and other text that requires more than one line.

To place a text field or a text area in a form, follow these steps:

1. With your cursor inside an existing form, choose Insert > Form > Text Field.

Tip

If you have enabled accessibility options, you'll be prompted to enter them before defining the field itself. See #75, "Defining a Form in Dreamweaver," for an explanation of these accessibility features.

2. After you place the text field, you can define the field attributes in the Property inspector (**Figure 76**). In the TextField field, enter a name that will help you remember the content of the field. In the Char width field, enter the number of characters that will display on a single line in a browser as a visitor enters data.

Figure 76 Defining a one-line text field, with input formatted using a CSS Class style.

3. In the Max Chars field, enter the maximum number of characters that can be entered into the field.

4. In the Init val field, enter text that will appear in the field in a browser before any user interaction. Sometimes form designers will include text like "your email goes here" in a field. Visitors then replace that content with their own entry.

continued on next page

5. In the Type options, choose Single line for a text field, and Multi line for a text area. If you choose Multi line, the Num Lines field appears in the Property inspector. Enter the number of lines that will display in the form (you cannot define a limit for the number of characters that are entered). In the Wrap pop-up menu, choose default, so text wraps in the browser window.

6. Enable the Password option to display content entered into the field as asterisks.

7. You can use the Class pop-up menu to attach a CSS Class style to the field.

Tip
See Chapter 8, "Formatting Text," and in particular #39, "Defining Inline Text Attributes with CSS," for a discussion of how to create and apply Custom Class styles.

As you define text field or text area attributes in the Property inspector, they display in the Document window.

#77 Placing Radio Buttons and Check Boxes

Radio buttons (aka option buttons) and check boxes represent two different ways to allow visitors to make selections from a set of options in a form. Radio (option) buttons force a visitor to choose *just one* from a set of options.

One frequently encountered situation in which radio buttons are the best way to collect information is when you are collecting credit card information from a purchaser. In that case, you want him or her to select one, and just one, type of card from a list of cards you accept.

On the other hand, check boxes (aka option boxes) allow visitors to choose, or not choose, any number of options. For instance, you might ask a person filling out a form if they want to be contacted by email, phone, snail mail, or text messaging. If you want to allow them to choose any combination of these options (including all or none of them), use check boxes.

To place a check box in a form, follow these steps:

1. With your cursor inside an existing form, choose Insert > Form > Checkbox.

   Tip
   If you have enabled accessibility options, you'll be prompted to enter them—including a label—before defining the field itself. See #75, "Defining a Form in Dreamweaver," for an explanation of these accessibility features. Do enter a label (check boxes need text to tell visitors what they are checking, and generated labels do this well), the label will display to the left or right of the check box.

2. After you place the check box, if you did not generate a label, you need to enter some text (normally to the right of the check box) that identifies what is being selected when a visitor selects the check box.

continued on next page

3. In the Property inspector, enter text and a description (such as Email, or Phone Contact) in the Checkbox field. In the Contact me by area, select the Email and/or Phone check boxes. Then enter "Yes" in the Checked value field. There are different styles and systems for identifying and collecting data in check boxes, and if you are designing a form in conjunction with a database programmer, check with him or her on how to manage this.

4. Select one of the Initial state radio buttons to define whether the default state of the check box is checked or unchecked (**Figure 77a**).

Figure 77a Defining a check box.

Tip

You can use the Class pop-up menu to attach a CSS Class style to the field. See #39, "Defining Inline Text Attributes with CSS" for a discussion of how to create and apply Custom Class styles.

Radio buttons differ from check boxes in that they always are organized in groups. You never have a single radio button—if you are asking a multiple-choice question in your form, use a check box. The purpose of radio buttons is to compel a user to choose one from a group of options.

Because radio buttons are organized into groups, they are a little more complicated to define than other form fields. And because Dreamweaver is the ultimate Web design program, it includes a dialog that manages the whole process of defining a radio button group easily.

To create a radio button group, follow these steps:

1. With your cursor inside an existing form, choose Insert > Form > Radio Group. The Radio Group dialog appears (**Figure 77b**).

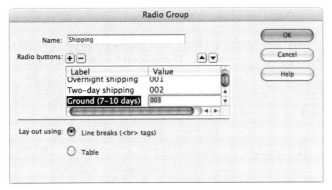

Figure 77b Defining a group of radio buttons.

2. In the Name field, enter a name that indicates *to you* the nature of the group of options. For example, if you are inquiring as to a type of shipping (Overnight, Two-day, Ground, etc.), you might call your group "Shipping."

3. In the Radio buttons area of the dialog, click the Label column. In the first row enter a label that will appear for visitors. Next to that label, in the Value column, enter the data that will be sent with the form. For example, a label might read "Two-day shipping" to make clear to a user what he or she is selecting. But the value sent to your shipping department might be "002"—an internal code that tells them how to handle and bill shipping.

4. In the second row, enter another Label and Value. Use the "+" button to add more rows of labels and values, and the "–" button to delete a selected row. Use the Up and Down arrow buttons to move selected rows up or down in the list of radio buttons.

continued on next page

Radio Button Group Names

Why don't you change the Radio Button information when you edit radio buttons? Because the Radio Button value defines the *group*. The values of individual radio buttons within a group can change, but the group name must be the same for all buttons in the group. You can test your radio button group in a browser; if you choose one option from within the group, all other options should become deselected. If that doesn't happen, you haven't assigned the exact same group name (in the Radio Button field in the Property inspector) to each radio button.

5. In the Lay out using area, choose either Line breaks radio button (for separated rows) or Table radio button (for rows designed in a table).

6. After you define the radio button options, click OK in the dialog to generate the radio group.

After you generate a radio button group, you can edit (or delete) radio buttons individually. If you want to add a radio button, you can copy and paste an existing one from the group and, in the Property inspector, change the Checked value (but not the Radio Button) content (**Figure 77c**).

Figure 77c Editing a single radio button.

#**78** Placing Lists/Menus and File Fields

Menus (sometimes called pop-up menus) allow visitors to choose one option from a pop-up menu. File Field forms allow visitors to attach files from their own computers to the form and send them along with the form.

List menus differ from menus in that list menus can be used to collect more than one choice from a list, while regular menus allow visitors to select just one item. List menus are usually a confusing way to collect data and are rarely used.

To create a menu, follow these steps:

1. With your cursor inside an existing form, choose Insert > Form > List/Menu.

   ### Tip
   If you have enabled accessibility options, you'll be prompted to enter them before defining the field itself. See #75, "Defining a Form in Dreamweaver," for an explanation of these accessibility features.

2. To create a list for the menu, click the List Values button in the Property inspector. The List Values dialog will appear. In the Item Label column, enter the text that will display in the menu (for example, Alaska). In the Value column, enter the value that will be collected and sent in the form (such as "AK"). Use the "+" button to add new items to the list and the "−" button to delete selected items. After you define the list, click OK (**Figure 78a**).

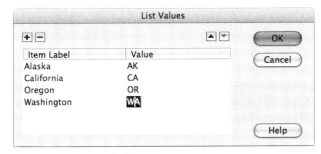

Figure 78a Defining a List/Menu.

continued on next page

3. After you generate a menu (or list), use the Property inspector to define additional features. You can add, delete, or edit actual menu (or list) items by clicking the List Values button in the Property inspector. This will open the List Values dialog where you can edit or change the order of menu (or list) options. You can change the initially selected option in the Property inspector by clicking an option in the Initially selected area. You can assign a CSS style using the Class pop-up menu (**Figure 78b**).

Figure 78b Choosing an initially selected option for a pop-up menu.

You can allow visitors to attach files to the form submission by inserting a file field in a form. Choose Insert > Form > File Field. You can define character width in the Property inspector.

Tip

Don't constrain the number of characters that visitors can use to define an uploaded file by entering a value in the Max Chars field in the Property inspector. There is no point to setting a limit on number of characters in an uploaded file's name.

#79 Using Hidden Fields

Hidden fields send information to a server that is not entered by the visitor filling out the online form. Hidden fields can be used to identify things like the page from which a form was sent.

Normally, you won't be creating hidden fields. It's more likely that they will be included in the HTML for a form that you download, connected to an existing server script. For instance, the form provided by Freeform to link to a search index database at their server includes several hidden fields (**Figure 79**).

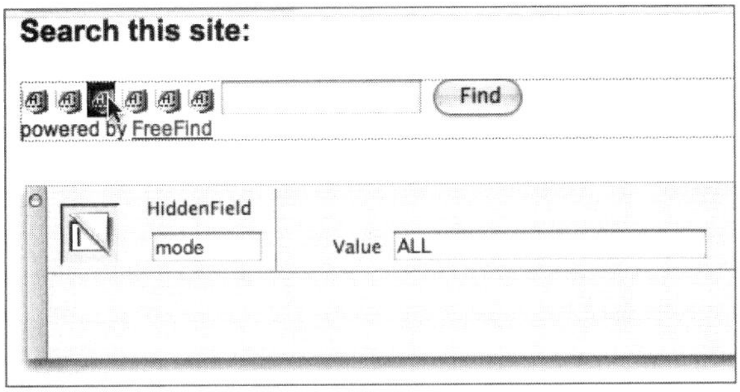

Figure 79 Examining a hidden field.

If you do need to create a hidden field in a form, choose Insert > Form > Hidden Field. The field, of course, does not display in the form; it appears only as an icon in the Document window. Enter a name for the field in the HiddenField field in the Property inspector, and enter a value in the Value field.

Don't Mess with Hidden Fields in Imported Forms

If a CGI script provider gives you HTML to create a form to send data to a server, they will likely include hidden fields. These hidden fields define how the data is processed at the server. So it's best if you don't edit or delete them.

#80 Placing Form Buttons

In order for form content to be sent to a server, there must be a Submit button in the form. Submit buttons are usually matched with a Reset button. The Reset button clears any data entered into the form, and allows the user to start fresh.

To place a button in a form, choose Insert > Form > Button. Use the Property inspector to define the button as a Submit or Reset button. In the Action area of the Property inspector, choose the Submit form or Reset form radio button (**Figure 80a**). No other settings are usually applied to Submit or Reset buttons, but a Submit button is essential if the form content is to be sent to a server.

Figure 80a Defining a Reset button.

You can define custom labels for either the Submit or Reset buttons by entering text in the Value field for either button. Don't get too fancy; visitors are used to seeing buttons that say something like "Submit" or "Reset." But if you enter different text in the Value field, that text will display in browsers and can be previewed in the Document window (**Figure 80b**).

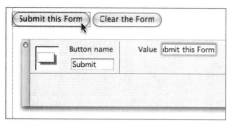

Figure 80b Creating a custom label for a Submit button.

#81 Defining Form Actions

Form Actions define how the data in a form is sent to a database on a server. Form actions are defined in the Property inspector with the *form*—not any specific form field—selected.

Tip
To select a form, click the dashed red line defining the form border. Or, click the <form> tag in the tag area on the bottom of the Document window.

The three important fields in the Property inspector for a form are the Action, Method, and Enctype fields. What you enter into these fields is determined by how the programmer (who set up the script and database to which the form data is being sent) configured the database and scripts at the server. Normally, Method is usually set to Post, but can sometimes be set to GET; this again depends on how data is transferred to the server, and is defined by how the server is configured. The Action field contains the URL of the Web page at the server that has the script that will manage the data.

Enctype, short for encryption type, is sometimes used to define how characters are interpreted and formatted. Your server administrator will tell you what, if any, enctype coding is required for forms to be processed by your server.

Since form actions are determined by the settings at your server, the information you enter into the Property inspector is provided by your server administrator. In the case of forms designed to match server scripts, those forms normally come with Action settings defined (**Figure 81a**).

Sending Form Content via Email—Pro and Con

The easiest way to collect form content is to have the content sent to an email address. This is the model used in this technique. The advantage is that it requires no scripting on your part. The downside is that it requires the person submitting the form to have an installed email client on his or her system. Although many users who have Internet access on their system have an email client as well, people using public computers at schools or libraries will not have access to email clients. For some applications, this is a problem.

Figure 81a Inspecting form action settings provided by a server administrator—in this case the Freefind search engine.

If you want to collect data in a form and have it sent to an email address, you can do this easily without having to work with additional server configuration or scripts. In the Action field, enter mailto:(your email address). From the Method pop-up menu, choose POST. In the Enctype field, enter text/plain (**Figure 81b**).

Figure 81b Defining an action that will send form content to an email address—in this case, mine!

CHAPTER FIFTEEN

Adding Animation and JavaScript

Animated and interactive Web pages are more dynamic, more active, and often more effective than static pages. *Animation* refers to page elements moving on the page. *Interactivity* means that objects on the page react when a visitor performs an action at a Web site. A box drops from the top of the browser window informing visitors of exciting news. A button changes color when a visitor hovers a mouse cursor over it. A sound goes off when a visitor clicks a button. These and many other animated and interactive elements can be generated right in Dreamweaver.

Dreamweaver generates animation and interactivity through something called *behaviors*. These behaviors mainly use Java-Script—a coding language that enables animation and interactivity. Small (relatively small, compared to most programming) scripts become part of the page code.

Dreamweaver generates behaviors using the Behaviors panel. In the Behaviors panel, you define two elements to every action: events and actions. *Events* trigger *actions*. An event might be a page opening. Or closing. Or a visitor hovering a mouse cursor over an object on the page. An action is generated by an event. Examples of actions include an image changing, a pop-up window opening, or a sound going off.

Many behaviors are defined interactively in the Behaviors panel—you choose from a list of possible events, and then choose an associated action. Other animated and interactive elements in Dreamweaver can be generated from the main menu in the Document window.

#82 Defining Browsers for Behaviors

JavaScript is interpreted by browsers, but some browsers don't support all the Dreamweaver-generated JavaScript. For this reason, the first step in defining most behaviors is to identify the browsing environment you are designing for. Browsers like Safari, Firefox, and Internet Explorer have built-in support for JavaScript. Older browsers and older versions of Internet Explorer do not support as much JavaScript as newer browsers.

By default, Dreamweaver displays only behaviors that work in nearly all browsers. If you accept this default setting, your set of available behaviors is quite restricted. And, in most cases, unnecessarily so. Very few Web surfers are still cruising the Web with Netscape Navigator 4.0—the default setting in Dreamweaver.

To change the default set of available behaviors, click the "+" button in the Behaviors panel. Select Show Events For from the pop-up menu, and then select one of the available browsers and browser versions (**Figure 82**).

Figure 82
Accessing behaviors that work in Internet Explorer 6.0.

Dreamweaver's set of available browsers is oddly out of date. However, Internet Explorer 6 is a de-facto standard that most other browsers adhere to, and so behaviors that work in Internet Explorer 6 are likely to work in other browsers.

Tip

If you want to detect the browser used by a visitor, and direct that visitor to another page if their browser does not support your behaviors, you can do so with behaviors that check browser compatibility. These behaviors are explained in #96, "Checking Browser Compatibility."

#83 Creating a Timeline

Frames and Keyframes

Timeline animation uses an interface and terminology similar to Flash animation. Timelines use the metaphor of *frames*—referring to the way animation in movies is generated by a rapid display of frames. In a timeline, animation is generated between *keyframes*. You define the location of specific keyframes (minimum of two), and then Dreamweaver generates the content of the in-between frames to provide a smooth, transitional animation between the two keyframes.

Timelines appear in a browser as an animated box that moves across, up and down, or diagonally on top of a Web page. Timelines often appear when a page opens—displaying content and providing an animated component to a page.

Timelines consist of a layer and a JavaScript that defines where and how the layer will move. The path that defines where the layer will move to and from is the *line* in Timeline. The *time* element is defined by how fast (measured in frames per second) the layer moves along the line.

The first step in creating a timeline is to place a layer on the page in the Document window.

1. Choose Insert > Layout Objects > Layer. Format the layer, and place images and/or text inside the layer. This is the content that will move on the page.

   Tip
   See Chapter 7, "Page Layout with CSS Layers" for a full exploration of how to create and format layers.

2. Choose Modify > Timelines > Add Object to Timeline. The Timelines panel will appear. When the timeline is first generated, it consists of 15 frames. The keyframes define the start and end positions of the animation (**Figure 83a**).

First keyframe   Last keyframe

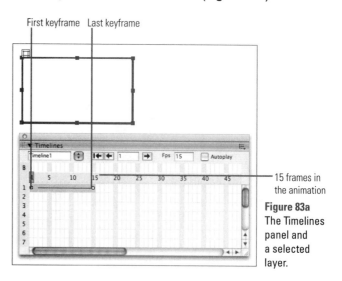

15 frames in the animation

Figure 83a
The Timelines panel and a selected layer.

3. With the first keyframe selected in the Timelines panel, drag the selected frame to the position on the page of the animation (or even off the page if you want the timeline to move onto the page from off the page) (**Figure 83b**).

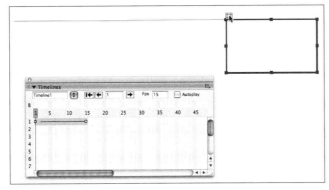

Figure 83b Placing the start point for a timeline animation.

4. In the Timelines panel, click the second (right) keyframe. With the second keyframe selected, drag the layer in the Document window to the end point for the animation (**Figure 83c**).

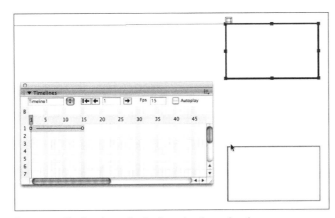

Figure 83c Placing the end point for a timeline animation.

continued on next page

#83: Creating a Timeline

Note

After you define the positions for the first and last keyframes in your timeline, a line appears in the Document window indicating the path the animation will take.

5. With the layer still selected in the Document window, you can define timeline attributes in the Timelines panel. Select the Autoplay check box to launch the timeline when the page is opened in a browser. Select the Loop checkbox to have the timeline repeat as long as the page is open. The default fps (frames per second) rate is 15. To slow down the animation, enter a lower value in the Fps field in the Timelines panel.

6. At any point in the process, you can edit the content of the layer itself—change the background color, add or change an image, or add text.

7. Test the timeline in a browser. You can adjust timeline features in the Timelines panel.

A very complex timeline might include more than fifteen frames. You can extend the length of a timeline by dragging the final keyframe in the Timelines panel (**Figure 83d**).

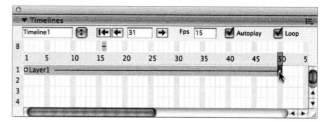

Figure 83d Extending the length of a timeline.

Complex timelines can include more than two keyframes. You can add a keyframe to a timeline by right-clicking/Ctrl-clicking any frame that is not a keyframe in the Timelines panel, and choosing Add Keyframe from the context menu (**Figure 83e**).

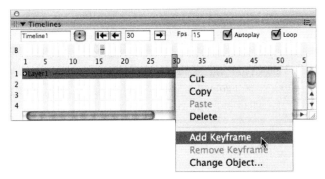

Figure 83e Adding a keyframe.

With a keyframe added, click that keyframe and move the layer in the Document window to the location where it will appear at that point in the animation (**Figure 83f**).

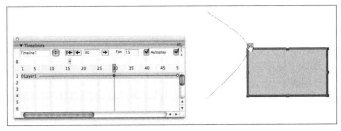

Figure 83f Positioning an added keyframe.

#**84** Opening a Browser Window

They're often called pop-ups—those little browser windows that open when you load a page in your browser, or when you activate the window by some action on the Web page. In Dreamweaver's terminology, they are referred to as *browser windows*, which is actually an accurate description of what most people call pop-ups.

The first step in creating a behavior that will open a browser window is to create a special Web page that will appear in that browser window. Since this page is likely to be displayed in a small browser window (you will be defining the size of that browser window as part of the behavior), you should design a page that will work well in a small browser window (**Figure 84a**).

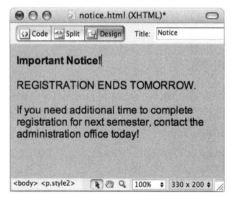

Figure 84a Preparing a small Web page to appear in a browser window.

With the Web page that will open in a new browser window prepared and saved, follow these steps to define the window:

1. From the Behaviors panel, click the "+" button and choose Open Browser Window from the list of behaviors (**Figure 84b**). The Open Browser Window dialog will open.

Figure 84b Choosing the Open Browser Window behavior.

2. In the URL to display field, navigate to or enter the Web page that will open in the new browser window.

3. Use the Window width and Window height fields to define the size of the browser window.

4. The display options available in the Attributes section of the Open Browser Window dialog are generally *not* enabled—the new browser window that pops up is usually displayed without features like a navigation toolbar or status bar. So, leave these options deselected.

continued on next page

Open Browser Window Trigger

By default, the open browser window behavior uses the page loading as the triggering event. In other words, the new browser window opens as soon as a visitor opens the launching page in his or her browser.

5. A Window name will be helpful as you edit this behavior. Enter a name in the Window name field, and click OK in the Open Browser Window dialog (**Figure 84c**).

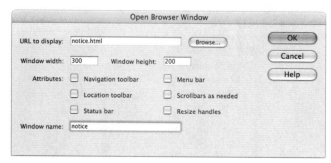

Figure 84c Defining an open browser window behavior.

Test your new browser window behavior by opening the page that launches it in a browser (**Figure 84d**).

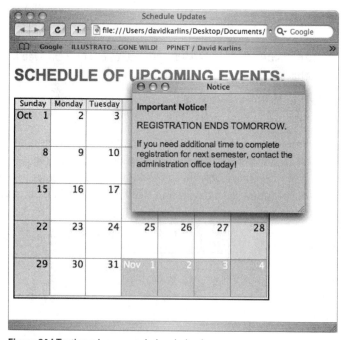

Figure 84d Testing a browser window behavior.

You can change the triggering event. For example, you can have a visitor click on specific text to open the new browser window. To do this, follow these steps:

1. In the Behaviors panel, click the Open Browser Window behavior in the list. Click the "–" button to delete this behavior. You will define a new behavior that will launch the new browser window using a different event (**Figure 84e**).

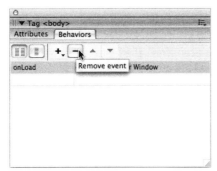

Figure 84e Deleting a browser window behavior.

2. Enter text on your page that will serve as a link to open the new browser window. In the Property inspector, enter the pound symbol ("#") in the Link field to create a self-referring link. This will display the text as a link, even though the result of clicking the link will be defined by a behavior (**Figure 84f**).

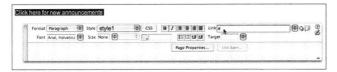

Figure 84f Preparing text to trigger an open browser window event.

continued on next page

Events and Actions

Behaviors have *events* and *actions*. The event is what triggers the behavior. The action is what happens.

Different events might trigger the same action—in this case, displaying a customized browser window.

Unfortunately, at this particular moment in the Macromedia to Adobe transition, a complete list of Dreamweaver 8 behavior events is not easily accessible from Adobe. However, a substantial list of behavior events is available in *Macromedia Dreamweaver 8 for Windows and Macintosh: Visual QuickStart Guide* (Peachpit Press, 2006), or you can search for online tutorials and lists of Dreamweaver 8 behavior events available from various Web sites.

Many events are pretty much self-descriptive. The onClick event, for example, obviously means the behavior is triggered when you click the selected object on the page. The onLoad event triggers behaviors when a page is loaded.

3. With the text you defined as a self-referring link in step 2 selected, define an Open Browser Window behavior just as you did in steps 1 to 5 earlier in this technique. However, this time—because you had link text selected—the default triggering event is not onLoad (page opens) but onClick (when the selected text is clicked).

If onClick is not set as the triggering event, you can select that from the first column pop-up menu in the Behaviors panel. Or, if you want to use a different triggering event (such as onMouseOver—when a visitor hovers a mouse cursor over the selected text), you can choose a different event from the first column pop-up menu in the Behaviors panel (**Figure 84g**).

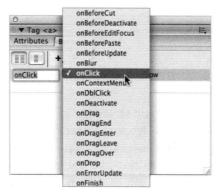

Figure 84g Defining onClick as the triggering event for an open browser window event.

#85 Designing a Pop-up Window

Pop-up messages present dialogs with information, and require a visitor to OK them before they will go away (**Figure 85a**).

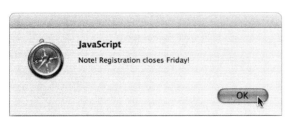

Figure 85a A pop-up dialog.

To create a pop-up message that displays a dialog, follow these steps:

1. If you want the pop-up to appear when the page loads, click the Body tag in the tag bar on the bottom of the Document window. If you want the pop-up to be triggered by clicking (or applying some other action to) text or an image, select the text or image.

2. In the Behaviors panel, click the "+" button to activate the list of available behaviors, and choose Popup Message (**Figure 85b**).

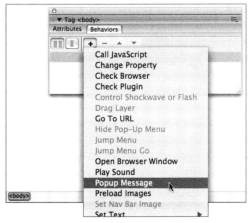

Figure 85b Selecting the Popup Message behavior with the body tag selected in the Tag bar.

continued on next page

#85: Designing a Pop-up Window

Pop-ups vs New Browser Windows

If you're looking for instructions on how to create those little windows that pop up with content on top of a Web page when you open it, refer to #84, "Opening a Browser Window." What many people refer to as pop-ups are actually new browser windows.

3. In the Popup Message dialog, enter the message visitors will see when the pop-up message is triggered (**Figure 85c**). Then click OK.

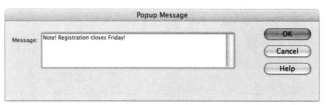

Figure 85c Entering a pop-up message.

4. Test the pop-up by previewing the page in a browser.

5. If you want the pop-up message to be triggered by clicking (or performing another action on) link text or an image, select that image before generating the pop-up behavior. If it is difficult to tell what object you have selected, you can select the object in the Tag bar, or verify that the object is selected in the Tag bar. Choose a triggering event like onClick from the Events column in the Behaviors panel (**Figure 85d**).

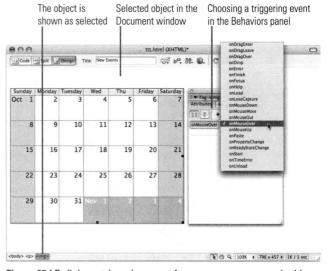

Figure 85d Defining a triggering event for a pop-up message—in this case, when a visitor hovers over the image, the pop-up appears.

#86 Validating Form Data

Chapter 14, "Collecting Data in Forms," explains how to design forms and manage form data. In this technique, I'll show you how to use scripts to test form input before it is submitted to a server.

For example, if you are collecting a U.S.-style zip code in a form field, you can test the information entered by a visitor to make sure they've entered numbers, not letters. If you require a visitor to provide an email address before submitting the form, you can make this a required field. If a visitor attempts to submit a form that does not meet validation rules, he or she will see a dialog explaining the problem, and directing him or her to provide required data (**Figure 86a**).

Figure 86a Attempting to submit a form that does not match validation rules.

Validation Scripts Are Client-Side Scripts

If you are familiar with how forms data is managed, you know that some data is sent to a remote server for processing, while other data is processed in the visitor's browser using JavaScript. A jump menu, for instance, processes a visitor's choice of a navigation link, and opens that page in a browser window. This is a *client-side* script.

Scripts that manage data sent to and processed at a remote server are referred to as *server-side* scripts. A query to a search box, for example, involves sending that query to a remote server, where the query content is matched with an index of site content and a results page is produced.

Validation scripts are usually applied to forms that collect data to be sent to a server. For example, you might test a search box query to make sure there is something entered in the box before sending the data to a server. In this case, the validation script that tests the field for content is a client-side script, while the script that processes the data at the search engine server is a server-side script.

To define validation scripts for a form, open the page containing the form, and follow these steps:

1. In the Behaviors panel, click the "+" button and choose Validate Form. The Validate Form dialog will open. The dialog displays all testable form fields in any forms on the open page (**Figure 86b**).

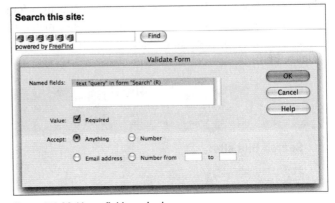

Figure 86b Making a field required.

Tip
Some form fields, like check boxes and radio button groups, are not validatable. They are either selected or deselected (in the case of check boxes) or one button in the set is selected (in the case of radio buttons).

2. Select one of the available fields on the page (if there is more than one) to define validation rules for that field.

3. To make a field required, select the Required check box in the Value area.

4. In the Accept area of the Validate Form dialog, choose among the four options.

   - Anything: Choose this option when a field is required, but any combination of letters, numbers, or other characters can be entered in the field.

- Number: Choose this option when only a number is accepted.

- Email address: Choose this option to constrain the field entry to something that *looks like* an email address. Email addresses are not actually tested, but visitors have to enter texts with an "@" symbol that appears to be an email address.

- Number from: Choose this option to restrict data to a value that falls between the numbers you enter.

#87 Attaching Sounds to Events

Used with discretion, sounds can liven up a Web site. A small, two-second-long chime sound or a doorbell sound might be inviting when visitors arrive at your site. You can assign sounds to go off when a page opens.

Sound files associated with opening a Web page should be small. Otherwise, by the time the sound file downloads and plays, the visitor will be well into (or out of) interacting with your page, and the experience will be one of a noise going off apparently at random. Also, sound files associated with page events should be in an accessible format. Small and accessible formats are WAV, MIDI, and AIFF.

To embed a sound event that opens when a page loads, click the "+" button at the top of the Behaviors panel, and choose Play Sound. The Play Sound dialog will open. In the Play sound field, navigate to a sound file using the Browse button, and select a sound file to play when the page opens (**Figure 87a**).

Figure 87a Embedding a sound.

By default, the event that triggers the sound will be the page loading. If another event is defined, for some reason, choose onLoad from the pop-up menu in the Event column of the Behaviors panel (**Figure 87b**).

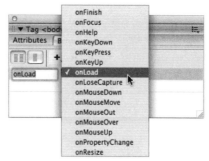

Figure 87b Assigning onLoad as the event for a sound file.

#88 Creating a Rollover

Rollover images change their display when a visitor hovers over the image. Rollover images are often, but not necessarily, used as links. There are always two images in a rollover—the original image that displays before a visitor rolls over the image, and the rollover image that displays when a visitor rolls over the image with his or her mouse.

The main work in preparing a rollover is to prepare two identically sized images. The rollover image displays in the *same box* as the original image. And if the rollover image has different dimensions than the original image, the rollover image will distort to fill the original image box.

With two same-sized images prepared, follow these steps to create a rollover:

1. Choose Insert > Image Objects > Rollover Image. The Insert Rollover Image dialog will appear (**Figure 88**).

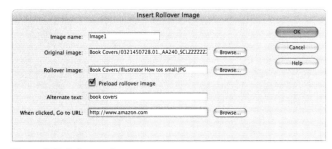

Figure 88 Defining a rollover.

2. You can accept the default image name in the Image name field; this is used for scripting.

3. Use the Browse button in the Original image field to locate and select an original image.

4. Use the Browse button in the Rollover image field to locate and select a rollover image.

continued on next page

Test Rollovers in a Browser

Rollovers depend on JavaScript that cannot be managed in the Dreamweaver Document window. Test rollovers by choosing File > Preview in Browser, and selecting an available browser.

5. Leave the Preload rollover image check box selected; this will ensure that visitors don't have to wait for the rollover image to download when they hover a mouse cursor over the original image.

6. If you want your rollover to serve as a link, enter a URL in the When clicked, Go to URL field, or use the Browse button to locate a link target in your Web site.

7. You can enter alternate text to make the rollover accessible to visitors with reader software or with image display disabled in their browsing device. When you have defined the rollover, click OK.

#**89** Creating an Interactive Navigation Bar

Interactive navigation bars generated by Dreamweaver use four different image buttons. One button displays as a typical static button on the page. The second button displays when a visitor hovers a mouse cursor over the button. The third displays when a visitor clicks the button. The fourth image displays when a visitor hovers a mouse cursor over the button (while in down state).

This means that you need four versions of every button you use in a navigation bar. If your navigation bar has four options, for example, you need sixteen buttons (four versions of each button).

To create a navigation bar, follow these steps:

1. In the Dreamweaver Document window, choose Insert > Image Objects > Navigation Bar. The Insert Navigation Bar dialog will open.

2. Each Navigation Bar Element is a four-state button. Each button is defined separately, as a four-image element. Enter the name of the first button in the Element Name box, and use the four browse buttons to navigate to and select the four button states for the first button.

3. Enter alternate text in the Alternate Text box to provide accessibility for visitors who will not see the button.

4. In the When clicked, Go to URL field, enter the link target for the button, or use the browse button to navigate to and select a target file in your site. You can choose _blank from the in pop-up menu to open the link in a new browser window.

5. Leave the Preload images check box selected so that images that display in alternate button states are downloaded and ready to display when a visitor hovers a mouse cursor over or clicks the button.

6. In the Insert pop-up menu, choose between Horizontally (a button bar running across the top or bottom of a page) and Vertically (a button bar running down the left side of the page). The Use tables check box generates tables to lay out the navigation bar. This is generally helpful unless you have already defined a table structure for the navigation bar.

continued on next page

Button Creation

Dreamweaver doesn't create these buttons. For that, you'll need to use a design program like Adobe Illustrator, and save (export) the button images as Web-compatible GIF, JPEG, or PNG image files.

For an extensive survey of how to use techniques like slicing to quickly generate Web-compatible images in Adobe Illustrator, see *Adobe Illustrator CS2 How-Tos: 100 Essential Techniques* by David Karlins (Adobe Press, 2006).

Do You Really Need Four Button States?

Here's a little secret: You might not need to create four different versions of the buttons in your navigation bar. If you create three, or even just two versions of each button, you can rotate or alternate buttons, so you use one or two of them twice.

You can maintain the dynamic interactivity of the navigation bar, even with just two versions of each button. So, for example, you can use one button for normal display and clicked state, and the second button for both the rolled over, and the rolled over when down states.

Astute visitors will appreciate the nuance and complexity of four different versions of each button—one for each state. But in many cases, two versions of each button is sufficient for a nice navigation bar.

7. When you have defined the first button, *do not click OK*. You have more buttons to define (**Figure 89a**).

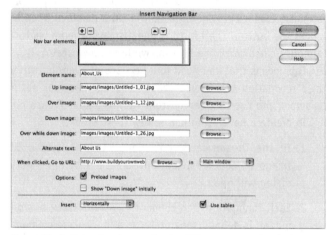

Figure 89a Defining four images for the different states of a single button in a navigation bar.

8. After you define the four states of your first button, click the "+" button in the Insert Navigation Bar dialog to add a second button. Define the second button. Continue defining four states for each button in your navigation bar.

9. You can use the up and down arrow buttons at the top of the dialog to move selected elements up or down in the list of elements. By moving different buttons up or down in the list of elements, you can change the order in which the buttons appear in a navigation bar (if, for example, you decide you want the button that links to your Home page at the top of the navigation bar). When you define all the buttons in the navigation bar, click OK to generate the navigation bar (**Figure 89b**).

Figure 89b Moving a button element down in the list.

You can't test the navigation bar in the Dreamweaver Document window. For that, you need to preview the page in a browser. Choose File > Preview in Browser and, if you have more than one browser configured, choose from the available browsers. After the navigation bar is generated, each (four-state) button is a distinct Behavior (or actually a set of behaviors). To edit any of the navigation bar buttons, select the button, and then double-click any of the actions (the left column) in the Behaviors panel to access a dialog to edit that button (**Figure 89c**).

Figure 89c Editing a navigation bar button.

#90 Generating a Photo Album

Dreamweaver Commands

The technique explored here for generating a photo album involves the Dreamweaver Commands menu. The Command menu allows you to record and playback sets of keystrokes. These recorded commands can streamline processes you repeat often.

In addition, the Commands menu includes a few prepackaged sets of keystrokes, like the one that generates a photo album.

Dreamweaver 8 includes a macro that will convert the images in a folder into a photo album. The result is a Web page with generated thumbnails of each image in the folder, and a set of pages with navigation links displaying full-sized versions of each image (**Figure 90a**).

Figure 90a Viewing a Dreamweaver-generated slideshow.

The macro that generates a photo album launches Fireworks 8, so you need Fireworks 8 installed on your computer to make this work. You also need to organize all the photos you want to include in the photo album (and *just* those photos) in a single folder. The photos must be in a Web-compatible format. Normally photos are best presented in JPEG format, but GIF and PNG files can also be used.

With your image files in a folder, follow these steps to generate a photo album:

1. From the Commands menu, choose Create Photo Album. The Create Web Photo Album dialog will appear.

2. Enter a title for the album in the Photo album title field.

3. Use the Subheading info and Other info fields to enter additional information that will display on pages that present the photos.

4. In the Source images folder field, enter (or browse to and select) the folder with the images that will be included in the photo album.

5. In the Destination folder field, enter (or browse to and select) the folder where the files generated for the photo album will be saved.

Tip

To smoothly integrate the slideshow into your Web site, designate a folder in your current Dreamweaver Web site as the target folder for generated files.

6. From the Thumbnail size pop-up menu, choose a size for the small thumbnails that will display on the home page of the slide show. Select the Show filenames check box if your filenames are descriptive and will add to the value of the presentation.

7. In the Columns field, enter the number of columns for the table that will be generated to display the thumbnails of your photos—on the slideshow home page.

8. In the Thumbnail format and Photo format pop-up menus, choose a level of quality for the generated images. Higher-quality images, of course, look better. But they download more slowly.

9. In the Scale field, you can adjust the scale of the full-sized photos in the slideshow. The default setting of 100% displays the images at their original size.

10. The Create navigation page for each photo check box generates a page for each image, with a navigation bar on top that allows viewers to see the previous or next image, or return to the photo album home page.

continued on next page

Dreamweaver's Photo Album Feature Requires Fireworks

There are two elements of creating a photo album. You need to generate Web pages to display pictures—Dreamweaver can do that very well. But you also need to do substantial photo editing. From the original photos, thumbnails need to be generated, along with full-sized Web images. Dreamweaver does not have that level of photo editing capacity. Therefore, the Dreamweaver photo album macro launches Fireworks, the companion image editing program that—in the Macromedia era—was packaged with Dreamweaver.

Other programs, including Adobe Photoshop, also have full-featured photo-album–generating macros.

#90: Generating a Photo Album

11. After you have defined the photo album, click OK (**Figure 90b**).

Figure 90b Preparing to generate a photo album.

After Dreamweaver (and Fireworks) generate the photo album (and this takes a while), the photo album will appear in the Dreamweaver Document window as a file, saved as index.htm, in the folder you designated (in step 5 above) as the target location for the slideshow files (**Figure 90c**).

Figure 90c A finished photo album.

You can edit and format the content of the generated photo album and slideshow to make both the album home page and the slideshow pages more attractive.

#91 Creating a Pop-up Menu

Pop-up menus appear when a visitor hovers over an image on your site. That image is usually a navigation button, designed in a program like Adobe Illustrator (**Figure 91a**). I've paid a hundred bucks for a pop-up menu generator that wasn't any better than the one you get with Dreamweaver for free.

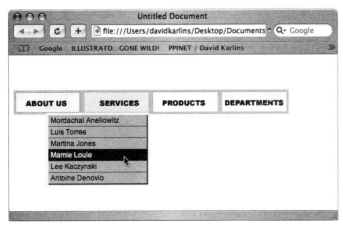

Figure 91a Hovering a mouse cursor over a Dreamweaver-generated pop-up menu.

In order to generate pop-up menus using Dreamweaver behaviors, you need to start with an image-based navigation bar. Design (or get a friend or professional to design) a set of navigation buttons that will fit together as a navigation bar, and place them on your page.

With at least one button in place, you can generate a pop-up menu with links. To do this, follow these steps:

1. Click the image button that will serve as the anchor for your pop-up menu. In the Behaviors panel, click the "+" button and choose Show Pop-Up Menu. The Show Pop-Up Menu dialog will appear, with the Contents tab selected.

continued on next page

Fireworks and Pop-up Menus

Fireworks is a nice fit for Dreamweaver; the complex interactive objects you create there open easily in Dreamweaver. Other options for creating more complex pop-up menus include several dedicated pop-up window programs you can find and purchase online (usually they provide a testing trial period so you can see if you like them before buying).

That said, for many of us, the set of pop-up menu features in Dreamweaver is sufficient. The main drawback is that the pop-up menu generator in Dreamweaver does not actually create the main navigation buttons that anchor the pop-up menu. For that, Adobe has Illustrator—the ultimate button design package. Alternately, if you don't have Illustrator, you can produce navigation buttons in Photoshop or other bitmap editors.

2. In the Text field, enter the text that will display for the first item in the menu. In the Link field, enter the URL of the link activated by clicking this menu option. You can use the blue Browse for Folder icon to navigate to a file on your site, and choose that as the link target.

Tip

If you want the link to open in a new browser window, choose _blank from the Target pop-up menu.

3. Click the "+" button to add more text and links to the pop-up menu (**Figure 91b**).

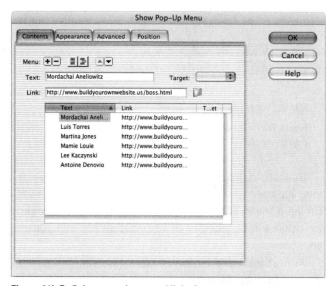

Figure 91b Defining menu items and links for a pop-up menu.

4. With the menu items and links defined, click the Appearance tab in the Show Pop-Up Menu dialog. If the images that compose your navigation bar are placed side-by-side at the top or bottom of the page, choose the Vertical menu option. If the images that compose your navigation bar have been placed top-to-bottom on the left side of the page, choose the Horizontal menu option.

5. Use the font and other formatting attributes to define the look of the text in your pop-up menu. An approximate preview in the dialog will guide your decisions (**Figure 91c**).

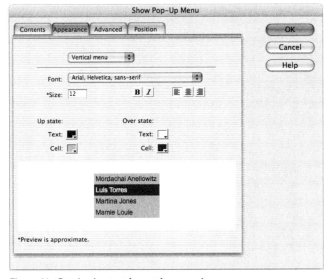

Figure 91c Previewing text format for menu items.

6. The Position tab in the Show Pop-Up Menu dialog allows you to customize how menu items extend to the right or left, above or below the original navigation bar image. The results you get using thedefault settings are generally clean and professional, but you can feel free to experiment and customize them.

7. After you define your pop-up menu, test it in a browser. To adjust the menu settings, select the button that anchors the pop-up menu, and double-click the Show Pop-Up Menu row in the Behaviors panel to reopen the dialog.

Getting Advanced

After you define appearance attributes of your pop-up menu, you can experiment, if you wish, with the options in the Advanced tab of the dialog. The default settings in this tab produce clean, professional menus, but if you are familiar with menu design, you can tweak the default settings.

CHAPTER SIXTEEN

Using Testing and Site Maintenance Tools

It ain't the glamorous side of Web design, but basic site mainte-nance like checking and fixing bad links, checking spelling, clean-ing up bad HTML imported with text from Microsoft Word, and checking browser compatibility and accessibility makes the dif-ference between a professional site, and—as long as we're in the vernacular here—crappy Web pages.

Dreamweaver provides a robust set of tools for making sure your site is error free, and ensuring that visitors' experience at your site is not marred with embarrassing misspelled words and busted links. This chapter will explore the most useful of those tools.

#92 Testing Links Sitewide

The dreaded "404 (page not found)" error is not an experience you want visitors to your Web site to go through. When visitors follow links on your site to pages that don't work—either on or outside your site—an error message appears in their browser, and—of course—they do not see the page that the link was supposed to open (**Figure 92a**).

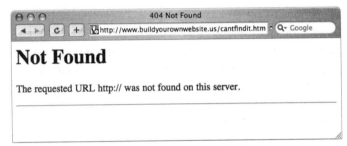

Figure 92a Broken links produce error messages in browsers.

Dreamweaver can easily and quickly test all the links in your site, both internal (links to files on your site) and external (links to pages and other files outside your site). Dreamweaver can also identify *orphan* pages—pages to which there is no link.

To test all links and identify orphan pages, follow these steps:

1. With or without a page open in the Document window, choose Site > Check Links Sitewide.

2. You can choose from the three reports in the Show pop-up menu in the Report window that opens after you check links (**Figure 92b**). Broken Links are bad links within your site. External Links are links to Web sites or pages outside your site that are no longer good. Orphaned Files are files to which there is no link from any page in your site.

Figure 92b Viewing broken links to files outside your site.

3. You can fix a broken link by double-clicking a link in the list of either the Broken Links or the External Links reports. The page with the bad link will open, and the link will be high-lighted. You can delete or update the URL for the bad link (**Figure 92c**).

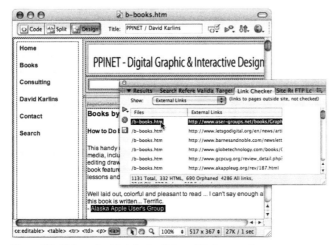

Figure 92c Fixing a bad link in the External Links report.

Should You Delete Orphan Pages?

Not all orphan pages are bad. For example, you might have a page that you have set up to be accessed by external links— links on other sites, not your own. That page would show up in the list of orphan pages because there is no link to it from *within* your Web site. That is obviously an orphan page you would not want to delete.

On the other hand, sometimes pages that are not the targets of any link in your site are obsolete and wasting server space, so it is often helpful to produce a list of such orphan pages.

#93 Checking Spelling

When you check spelling in Dreamweaver, you do so one page at a time. To check spelling for a page open in the Document window, select Text > Check Spelling. The Check Spelling dialog will open (**Figure 93a**).

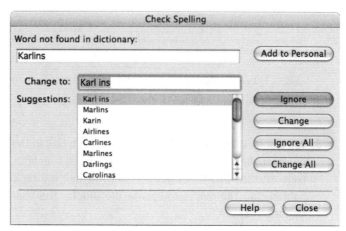

Figure 93a The Check Spelling dialog found a word it does not recognize.

If the spell checker identifies a word not found in Dreamweaver's dictionary, the word appears in the Word not found in dictionary field in the dialog.

You can click Ignore to ignore the word once. Or you can replace the spelling with a word selected from the Suggestions list or entered into the Change to field, and then click the Change button. Click Ignore All to ignore all instances of the unrecognized word, or click Change All to replace all instances of the unrecognized word with the replacement spelling in the Change to field. (**Figure 93b**).

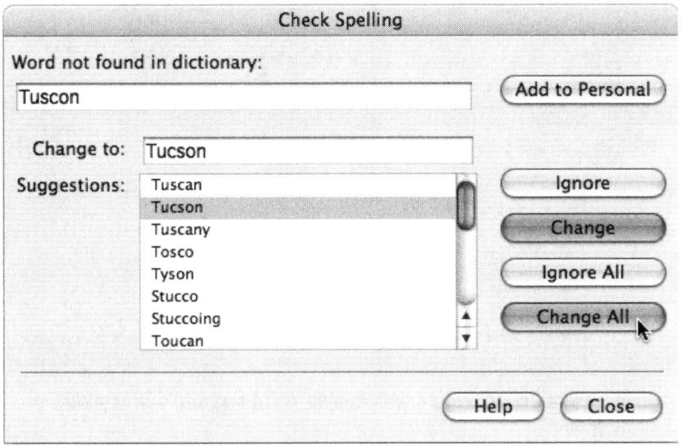

Figure 93b Fixing all instances of a misspelled word.

In addition to correcting or ignoring words, you can add them to your personal dictionary. When a word appears in the Word not found in dictionary field in the dialog, click the Add to Personal button.

Choosing Dictionaries for Different Languages

Dreamweaver comes with built-in dictionaries for over a dozen languages. Choose a language from the Check Spelling pop-up menu in the General category of the Preferences dialog. Access the Preferences dialog by choosing Edit (in Windows) or Dreamweaver (Mac) > Preferences.

#94 Cleaning Up Word HTML

Most text is created in Microsoft Word. There are a number of ways to convert that text to HTML. You can choose to save a Word file as HTML, and then open that HTML file in Dreamweaver and edit it, or you can copy and paste text from Word into a Dreamweaver document. If you choose File > Paste Special, the Paste Special dialog provides a number of options for how to handle Word formatting when text is copied from Word to Dreamweaver (**Figure 94a**).

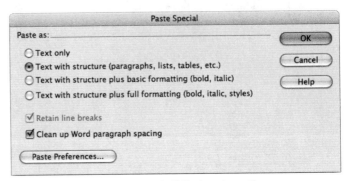

Figure 94a Options for pasting copied Word text into a Dreamweaver document.

Depending on the options you choose when importing Word text into Dreamweaver, the HTML that is generated will range from slightly flawed to really weird. If you elect to preserve all formatting from Word documents (which happens if you save a Word document as an HTML page and open it in Dreamweaver), the HTML code is full of proprietary Microsoft codes that make the page confusing to edit and format.

To clean up HTML pages with imported Word text, choose Commands > Cleanup Word HTML. The Clean Up Word HTML dialog will open (**Figure 94b**).

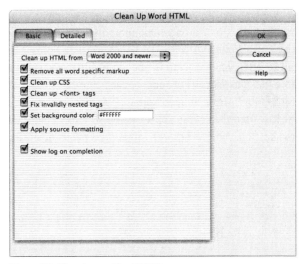

Figure 94b Cleaning up Word HTML.

Normally, you can accept the defaults in this dialog (all options are checked), and click OK. If you are using a pre-Word 2000 version of Microsoft Word, choose that version from the Clean up HTML from pop-up menu.

If you are curious as to what kind of nonstandard HTML is fixed by this process, or if you are an HTML and CSS coder and want to manage this process in detail, click the Detailed tab in the Clean Up Word HTML dialog. You can observe, or change, the fixes applied to Word HTML. After you click OK in the Clean Up Word HTML dialog, a dialog opens telling you what Word HTML was fixed in the process (**Figure 94c**).

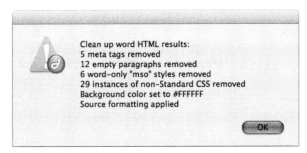

Figure 94c The report on what was fixed in the Word HTML.

The Paste Special dialog box that is available when you paste Word text into a Dreamweaver document provides a few levels of preserving formatting, ranging from preserving very little formatting from the Word document, to preserving almost all.

If you choose the Text only option in the Paste Special dialog, only text is pasted. This option allows you to reformat text in Dreamweaver, without worrying about formatting imported from Word. Choosing the text with structure plus full formatting (bold, italic, styles) option imports not only all formatting, but also style definitions (like Heading 1) that are converted in Dreamweaver to CSS styles.

#95 Adding Design Notes

Design Notes Are Editable

When you open a page that has attached Design Notes, the very same, editable, Design Notes dialog opens that you used to define the Design Note.

This allows you to edit a Design Note when you open the page to which it is attached. For instance, if you made a note to yourself (or other designers) that a page required approval, you might be authorized to remove that note when you make additional edits to the page.

If you are working on a Web site with others, or simply want to add "post-it" type notes to pages reminding yourself of things to fix, you can attach Design Notes to pages. Design Notes can be configured to open when a page is opened in Dreamweaver.

To add a Design Note to an open page, choose File > Design Notes. The Design Notes dialog will open (**Figure 95**). Here you can define a status from the Status pop-up menu. There are eight available status settings, including draft, final, and needs attention.

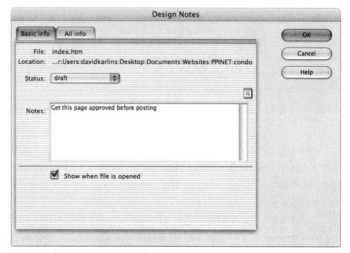

Figure 95 Defining a design note.

In the Notes area, enter any text you wish. Select the Show when file is opened checkbox to have the notes appear when you open a page for editing in Dreamweaver. These notes never appear in a browser.

Note
The All info tab in the Design Notes dialog does not enable any additional, easily defined notes options. It displays a Behaviors panel–type environment where you can see the options you selected in the Basic info tab. It is possible to generate additional JavaScript in this tab.

#96 Checking Browser Compatibility

Buried in the Dreamweaver Document toolbar is an icon that controls how Dreamweaver checks your Web pages to ensure compatibility with browsers. This icon also opens menus that produce reports on browser compatibility issues.

Dreamweaver can check your page to make sure it is compatible with any combination of Firefox, Internet Explorer for Windows, Internet Explorer for Mac, Mozilla, Netscape Navigator, Opera, and Safari. Several versions of each of these browsers are supported by this feature.

To define the browsers with which Dreamweaver will check your page for compatibility, click the Browser Check icon in the Document toolbar, and choose Settings (**Figure 96a**).

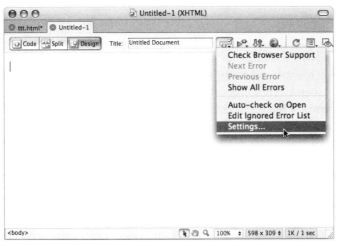

Figure 96a Accessing Browser Check settings in the Document toolbar.

Tip

If the Document toolbar is not visible, choose View > Toolbars > Document to display it.

The Settings selection will open the Target Browsers dialog. Here, you define which browsers, and which version of each selected browser, will be used to test your page. Choose browsers by selecting the check box next to the browser, and choose a version of that browser from the accompanying pop-up menu (**Figure 96b**).

Does Your Site Have to Be Compatible with *Every* Browser?

It's on you to assess your audience. If 5 percent of your visitors are viewing your site using Internet Explorer on a Mac, do you care if they see a lot of error messages? I would—5 percent can be a lot of people. The client who places the big order? The company that retains your services? Your family coming to see your wedding photos?

At the same time, making your site compatible with all major browsers reduces the number of behaviors you can use, and some other CSS formatting is also not supported by all browsers.

One flexible approach is to configure Dreamweaver to tell you about compatibility errors in various browsers. That way, if one feature doesn't work in one browser, you can set up your page so that the non-supported feature (like, perhaps, a CSS format applied to text) is not critical to getting content from the site.

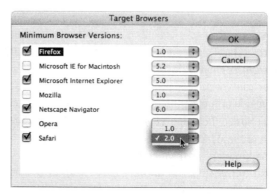

Figure 96b Defining the set of browsers for which Dreamweaver will test your page for compatibility.

After you OK the Target Browsers dialog, your pages will be tested for browser compatibility issues with the set of browsers you defined.

You can automatically check pages for browser compatibility issues by choosing Auto--check on Open from the Browser Check menu in the Document toolbar. Or, you can view a list of all browser compatibility issues in any open document by choosing Show All Errors from the menu. When you do this, a list of errors appears, telling you what features are not supported in different browsers (**Figure 96c**).

Figure 96c Viewing a list of browser compatibility issues for a page.

The list of browser compatibility issues that appears in the Target Browser Check window requires some familiarity with, or ability to decipher coding in order to interpret. The Description column explains the support issue, and the Line column identifies the line of coding in code view. If you know some HTML, you might be able to tweak the code yourself. Or even if you don't, you can often figure out what the problem is, and delete a feature from the description that appears in the Description column.

Using Testing and Site Maintenance Tools

#97 Testing Browsers for Media Support

Media files require plug-in software to be played in a browser. A large percentage of folks who browse the Web have downloaded and installed players for Windows Media, QuickTime, and Flash files.

On the other hand, not everyone has downloaded players that support all the main media file types. Dreamweaver generates a quick, easy behavior that will detect browsers that do not have a defined media player installed, and that can reroute these visitors to an alternate page in your site that does not require that particular plug-in to make the page work.

The behavior that tests a visitor's browser for plug-in support is triggered by a page loading in a browser window. To facilitate this happening correctly, select the <body> tag in the tag selection area on the left side of the status bar in the Document window generating the behavior (**Figure 97a**).

Figure 97a Selecting the <body> tag in the tag selection area.

Tip

By selecting the <body> tag before defining a behavior, you are allowing an action that affects the entire Web page (like loading the page in a browser) to be the triggering action for that behavior. See a more developed discussion of how Dreamweaver uses behaviors to generate JavaScript and other interactive and dynamic script and code, in Chapter 15, "Adding Animation and JavaScript."

Follow these steps to generate a behavior that will test browsers for plug-in support for a media player.

1. With the <body> tag selected in the open page tag selection area, click the "+" button in the Behavior panel, and choose Check Plugin (**Figure 97b**). The Check Plugin dialog will open.

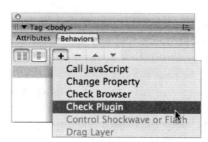

Figure 97b Initiating the Check Plugin behavior.

2. With the Select radio button selected, choose one of the available media types from the pop-up menu (**Figure 97c**).

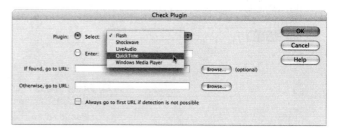

Figure 97c Choosing a plug-in to test for when the page is opened.

Tip

For all practical purposes, the plug-ins you can test for with a generated Behavior are constrained to the list in the Select pop-up menu. Theoretically, you could enter the name of another plug-in in the Enter field, but this option requires knowing exactly how to formulate the name of a plug-in in a way that generated JavaScript can manage it.

3. The If found, go to URL field is optional and typically not used. If the page to which you are applying the behavior is the page with the media that requires a plug-in, visitors who do have that plug-in will stay on this page by default.

4. In the Otherwise, go to URL field, enter the (full) URL of the alternate page that contains a version of the page content that does not require the selected plug-in. If the alternate page is a file in your Web site, you can navigate to and select that file with the Browse button.

5. Selecting the Always Go to first URL if detection is not possible checkbox opens the current page if the script that tests for a plug-in is not able to determine whether or not the plug-in is installed. Not infrequently, visitors have Flash or another plug-in installed, but the testing script is unable to determine this. If you select this check box, visitors will be diverted to the alternate page only if the testing script definitively determines that they do *not* have plug-in support for the selected media type. After you define the whole behavior, click OK (**Figure 97d**).

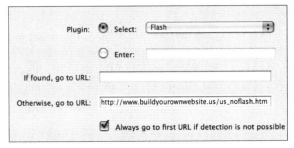

Figure 97d Assigning an alternate page to open if a visitor does not have Flash Player installed.

Have Your Plug-ins, and Your Accessibility Too!

If you want to include a lot of plug-in dependent media on your site, and have your site be highly accessible to visitors using different operating systems, viewing environments, and browsers, you should create alternate pages for pages that require plug-in support.

For example, if you have a page that features Flash buttons, Flash text, Flash video, and Flash animation, you might create an alternate page that has the same content, but just plain text buttons, HTML text, and no animation (just a JPEG, GIF, or PNG image). That alternate page would appear only when a visitor whose browser does not support Flash opens the page.

#98 Cleaning Up HTML

Why Does Dreamweaver Code Have to Be Cleaned Up?

The answer to this question is, in part, that often it does not. In #94, I discussed problems caused by integrating HTML generated by Microsoft Word into Dreamweaver. The biggest problem with Word-based content is that it often contains special, proprietary Microsoft markup tags that are not reliably interpreted by all browsers or operating systems.

But what about the HTML generated by Dreamweaver itself? It includes some errors as well. Why? Because when you apply, change, and delete formatting, for example, some code gets left behind.

Dreamweaver has a tool that examines and cleans up extraneous or sloppy code that inevitably results from a program that generates code based on things you do in Design view.

To clean up the HTML on an open Web page, choose Commands > Clean Up HTML. The Clean Up HTML/XHTML dialog will open (**Figure 98a**).

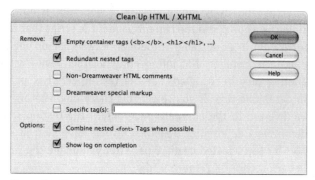

Figure 98a Cleaning up Dreamweaver-generated HTML.

The default settings in the Clean Up HTML/XHTML dialog will fix the kinds of HTML clutter that typically results from generated HTML code.

After you click OK, if you accepted the defaults, Dreamweaver produces a dialog that either tells you there was nothing to clean up, or identifies code that was cleaned up (**Figure 98b**).

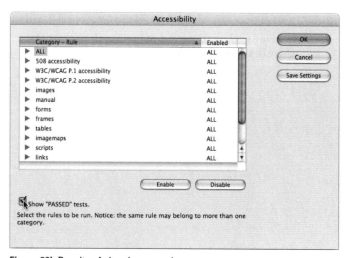

Figure 98b Results of cleaning up code.

Using Testing and Site Maintenance Tools

#99 Testing Accessibility

Dreamweaver 8 is configured so that, by default, when you insert elements like images, forms, or tables, you are prompted to enter accessibility attributes into dialogs. These accessibility options make your Web site accessible to visitors with a variety of disabilities.

Dreamweaver also generates reports that identify accessibility issues. These reports are helpful in ensuring that your site is accessible. They can also document the level of accessibility of your site, a requirement for some companies, organizations, and agencies that have policies mandating that their physical and virtual resources are accessible.

To generate an accessibility report, choose Site > Reports from the Document window (you do not need to have a document open to do this). The Reports dialog will open. From the Report On pop-up menu, choose Enter Current Local Site. From the set of check boxes, select Accessibility (**Figure 99a**).

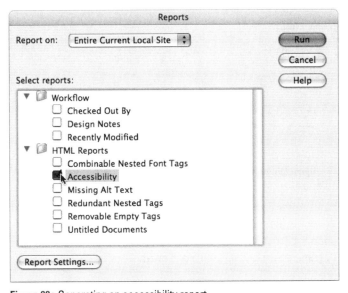

Figure 99a Generating an accessibility report.

Accessibility Issues

The most extreme impediment to visitors experiencing your Web site is lack of vision. Accessibility tools for vision-impaired visitors provide content that is read aloud by reader software—software that reads the content of the site aloud for vision-impaired visitors. Other accessibility issues range from color blindness to medical conditions that are exacerbated by using a mouse or viewing flashing light.

With the Accessibility report selected, you can click Report Settings to see a detailed set of accessibility tests that can be enabled or disabled. If you have been given a set of accessibility criteria to test for, you can fine-tune the testing process to produce a report that tests only those criteria. In most cases, the default test that checks all the features in your site is appropriate.

You probably will want to select the Show "PASSED" tests check box in the Accessibility dialog that opens when you click the Check Reports button. That way, you will learn what accessibility features your site *does* support (**Figure 99b**).

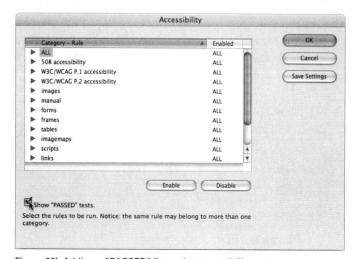

Figure 99b Adding a "PASSED" list to the accessibility report.

After you define the accessibility test, click Run in the Reports dialog. A list of accessibility problems will be produced. If you double-click a page in the Results column, that page opens in the Document window for editing (**Figure 99c**).

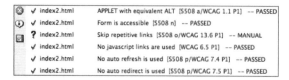

Figure 99c Opening a page with an accessibility issue.

#**100** Synchronizing Local and Remote Sites

Dreamweaver allows you to automatically update your local and remote sites. You can do this three ways:

- You can transfer all updated files from your local site (your own computer) to the remote site (the server). This is the standard operation for updating your Web site after editing it on your local computer.

- You can transfer all updated files from your remote site to your local site. There are a number of situations in which this is useful. For example, if your site has been updated using a different computer than the one you are working on, you can update the version of your Web site on your computer by downloading all newly edited files from the server.

- You can replace files on both the local and remote sites with the latest versions of the file.

You also have the option, when you synchronize sites, to upload (or download) all files, or selected files. If you want to synchronize only selected files, Shift-click or Command/Ctrl-click to select files for uploading in the Site panel before you synchronize sites (**Figure 100a**).

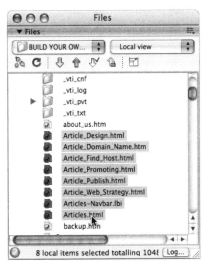

Figure 100a Selecting files in the Site panel for synchronization.

To synchronize your local and remote sites, follow these steps:

1. Choose Site > Synchronize Sitewide (a page does not have to be open to do this). The Synchronize Files dialog will open.

2. In the Synchronize pop-up menu, choose either your Entire site or Selected Local Files.

3. In the Direction pop-up menu, choose "Put newer files to remote" if you want to update your remote site. Choose "Get newer files from remote" if you want to update your local site. Choose "Get and Put newer files" if you want to update both your local and remote sites with the latest version of every file.

4. You can clean up your remote site by selecting the delete remote files not on local drive check box. This removes all files from the remote server that are not found in your local site. After you define the synchronize settings, click Preview (**Figure 100b**).

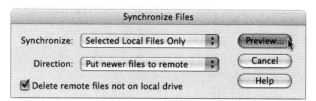

Figure 100b Defining synchronization settings.

In the Synchronize dialog, Dreamweaver generates a list of files that will be transferred. If Dreamweaver identifies a reason to hold off on synchronizing the site, "Resolve" will appear in the Action column of the Synchronize dialog.

Tip
Dreamweaver might flag a file to not synchronize if, for example, an older file is replacing a newer one.

Dreamweaver will prompt you to resolve an issue if *both* the remote and local versions of a file have been updated since you last synchronized. Right-click/Ctrl-click the word *Resolve* to choose a way to resolve the issue. Choose Change Action to Put from the context menu to upload the selected file. Choose Change Action to Get from the context menu if you are synchronizing sites by updating the local site. Other context menu options allow you to delete the file, ignore the selection, mark the file as synchronized (overriding the automatic synchronization process), or compare the local and remote versions (**Figure 100c**). When you OK the Synchronize dialog, files are transferred.

Figure 100c Resolving synchronization issues for a selected file.

Here's an example of how this would work: If you have updated your index.htm file on your local server, and another person working on your same site has updated the aboutus.htm file, and uploaded that file to the remote server, then this synchronization technique would replace the index.htm file at the remote server with the file from your computer, and replace the aboutus.htm file at your local computer with the file from the remote server.

When Would You Synchronize by Updating Both Local and Remote Sites?

Normally, you synchronize sites by updating your remote server with files you have edited on your local computer. But sometimes, you might want to update both your local and remote sites. This would be the case if you and another developer were working on a site together, and you wanted to download files he or she had updated at the server, and upload files you edited.

#100: Synchronizing Local and Remote Sites

Index

Index